# A Flick of Sunshine

# A Flick of Sunshine

*The Remarkable Shipwrecked, Marooned, Maritime*
*Adventures, and Tragic Fate of an American Original*

## Frederic B. Hill

### and

## Alexander Jackson Hill

LYONS
PRESS

*Guilford, Connecticut*

LYONS
PRESS

An imprint of Globe Pequot, the trade division of
The Rowman & Littlefield Publishing Group, Inc.
4501 Forbes Blvd., Ste. 200
Lanham, MD 20706
www.rowman.com

Distributed by NATIONAL BOOK NETWORK

British Library Cataloguing in Publication Information available

Library of Congress Cataloging-in-Publication Data available

ISBN 978-1-4930-6081-8 (cloth : alk. paper)
ISBN 978-1-4930-6082-5 (electronic)

♾️™ The paper used in this publication meets the minimum requirements of American National Standard for Information Sciences—Permanence of Paper for Printed Library Materials, ANSI/NISO Z39.48-1992.

*For Marty: For your unwavering love, support and dedication during this project and throughout the journey of life.*

*"Only a moment; a moment of strength, of romance, of glamour—of youth!*

A flick of sunshine *upon a strange shore, the time to remember, the time for a sigh, and good-bye!—Night—Good-bye . . . !"*
—FROM *YOUTH,* BY JOSEPH CONRAD (1898)

# Contents

## Contents

# PREFACE

*A FLICK OF SUNSHINE* IS THE STORY OF THE EXTRAORDINARY LIFE OF adventure and exploration of a still not fully charted globe by a young man of strong character and independence, considerable intellect, no little ambition, and that most admirable of traits, a sense of humor.

From his upbringing in a small but vibrant city of ships in Maine to shipwreck and survival on a few tiny islands in the Pacific Ocean, from running down glaciers in Alaska to persevering through the old boy network of the maritime world in search of his captain's papers, this book offers a compelling account of a determined young man and his challenging experiences and narrow escapes in the closing days of the majestic, square-rigged ships known as Downeasters.

The book was inevitable once my mother, Alex's grandmother, gave me several hundred letters of her father's older brother, Richard Willis Jackson. They are a remarkable treasure trove of an adventurous life before the mast. Given the fast-fading pencil scrawls of many of his letters, Alex and I sought to decipher and transcribe the documents in the mid-1990s, when Alex was in high school.

We completed that work in several months, producing a fifty-page document.

But it was not until I discovered a diary of Jackson's and had completed an account of Jackson's grandfather's shipbuilding venture in Bath, Maine—*Ships, Swindlers and Scalded Hogs* (Down East Books, 2016)—that I appreciated the broader context of Will Jackson's background and life choices. After the collapse of his family's shipyard—one of the most successful in Maine and the United States for a few years in the mid-nineteenth century—Jackson was drawn to the sea and a life of adventure.

~~~

The shipwreck and his experience in the Marshall Islands in 1884 alone warrant a full and fair accounting to the general public, especially with regard to the world of naval, maritime, and seafaring folk. Jackson's and the crew of *Rainier*'s travails after crashing on an unmarked reef in the vast Pacific Ocean were related in a compact book, *Wreck of the Rainier*, by Omar J. Humphrey, first mate of the ship, and by Jackson, who wrote two chapters of the book, though without credit.

Yet, of the twenty-eight original members aboard *Rainier*, all but two of whom survived the voyage, wreck, and extended stay in the islands, only Will Jackson went on to have a particularly remarkable career. Captain Samuel Morrison not only suffered a stroke after the shipwreck in the Marshall Islands, but most of his shipboard experiences were behind him, and he retired to Santa Clara, California. His maritime career had been one misadventure after another.

It is surprising that the Sewall shipbuilding firm in Bath gave Morrison command of their new ship *Rainier* after he had lost two ships, the most recent in January 1883 when another Bath-built ship *Oracle* encountered a hurricane rounding Cape Horn. The fact that only one sailor was lost in the two incidents, during which Morrison was credited with masterful sailing, may have preserved his reputation.

In his excellent book on Sewall shipbuilding, *Live Yankees*, William Bunting offered a telltale observation on the fate and fortunes of ship captains: "There were captains who retired after many years at sea and had never lost a ship. Doubtless, most of these men were very competent shipmasters, but . . . also very fortunate, such were the hazards of the sea. And there were other masters at least as competent and cautious who suffered disaster more than once. When the Sewalls suspected that one of their captains was of the unlucky sort, they found a way to be rid of them." Bunting saluted Will Jackson's heroic leadership of the rescue of the crew of *Rainier*, calling him "a smart young Mainer."

Humphrey, first mate on both *Oracle* and *Rainier,* did go on to command a number of schooners on the west coast after the Marshall Islands wreck.

Will Jackson's story turned out to be something else altogether—and that colorful, adventurous career, overcoming one challenge after another, surviving one narrow escape after another—is the focus of this book.

Richard Matthews Hallet also deserves credit for inspiring this book. A cousin of my mother, a nephew of Will Jackson, Hallet became just as enthralled as his uncle with the lure of exotic, far-off places and, no doubt, the lives of their mutual ancestors, Charles and William Donnell Crooker, leading shipbuilders in Maine in the mid-nineteenth century until costly swindles, bad investments, and deep distrust led to the end of their firm in 1854.

Despite a Harvard University and Harvard Law School education, plus a job offer from a prestigious New York admiralty law firm, Hallet devoted his life to adventure and writing in the first half of the twentieth century. He shipped out across the globe, trekked through the wilderness of Australia, shoveled coal on transatlantic steamers, served in the US Merchant Marine during World War I and reported on World War II. Based on his experience in wartime aboard merchant vessels and reporting, articles he wrote helped inspire establishment of the Maine Maritime Academy. In addition to his newspaper work and hundreds of short stories in popular magazines such as the *Saturday Evening Post* and *Harper's,* he authored five novels and an entertaining autobiography, *The Rolling World.*

I found the title to this work in a Colby College tribute to Hallet after his death in 1967—and a renewed respect for Joseph Conrad, one of Hallet's favorite authors, along with Jack London and Willa Cather. Conrad and Will Jackson were contemporaries, and had traveled many of the same sea lanes, and experienced strikingly similar challenges on the oceans of the world.

Conrad's voyages "opened the east to him," critic Morton Dauwen Zabel once wrote, of Conrad's use of "the strictest realism ... of his life as an exile and seaman, he had to learn, know, and accept his subject matter on its own terms before he could see it in terms of art."

Taking on his fourth language, Conrad, a native of Poland who spent many years in the French maritime service, did not write his early novel *Youth* until the age of thirty-one. It is not improbable to think that had Will Jackson found a longer period of "sunshine," given his extraordinary exploits, his convictions, and clear writing talent, that he may well have given good account of his very *real* experiences in a tolerably Conradian form.

It is fitting to close this introduction with an evocative excerpt from another Conrad novel, which Henry James called "the very finest and strongest picture of the sea and sea-life that our language possesses." It describes a return to normal after a dramatic, days-long and terrifying storm at sea.

> *This was the last of the breeze. It veered quickly, changed to a black south-easter, and blew itself out, giving the ship a famous shove to the northward into the joyous sunshine of the trade. Rapid and white she ran homewards in a straight path, under a blue sky and upon the plain of a blue sea.*
>
> *. . . The fear and anguish of these dark moments were never mentioned in the glowing peace of fine days. Under a low, grey sky, the ship, in close heat, floated upon a smooth sea that resembled a sheet of ground glass. Thunder squalls hung on the horizon, circled round the ship, far off and growling angrily, like a troop of wild beasts afraid to charge home.*
>
> *The invisible sun, sweeping above the upright masts, made on the clouds a blurred stain of rayless light. . . . At night, through the impenetrable darkness of earth and heaven, broad sheets of [lightning] waved noiselessly, and for half a second the becalmed craft stood out with its masts and rigging, with every sail and every rope distinct and black in the centre of a fiery outburst, like a charred ship in a globe of fire.*[1]

Frederic B. Hill      Alexander Jackson Hill
Arrowsic, Maine            San Francisco
March 2020

# CHAPTER ONE

# Ujae

THE ATOLL OF UJAE IN THE MARSHALL ISLANDS IN THE WEST-CENTRAL Pacific Ocean lies at latitude 9.08036, longitude 165.679413.

Sitting near the equator and slightly west of the International Date Line, the Marshall Islands were first thought to have been visited by Micronesian colonists in the second millennium B.C. They were first sighted by Spanish and Portuguese explorers in the 1520s, and were given their name by an English seafarer, John Marshall, in 1788.

The Marshall group of twenty-nine atolls and five single islands contains 2,100 small coral reefs and islets, covering seventy square miles of *land* area, but are spread out over 772,000 square miles of water, approximately one-quarter of the total area of the continental United States (3.1 million square miles).

Ujae, pronounced "oodge-eye" and often spelled Ujea, is a kite-shaped atoll consisting of a coral reef of twelve small islets that total a bit less than one square mile of land but enclose a lagoon of seventy-two square miles. Only the largest, Ujae, is inhabited: Its highest elevation is ten feet above sea level.

In the late nineteenth century, Ujae, like much of the Marshall Islands group, was not accurately charted on nautical maps.

At the end of the year 1883, in the days of the majestic three- and four-masted sailing ships known as Downeasters, a brand-new, two-thousand-ton, fully-rigged, three-masted ship christened *Rainier* was cruising through the aqua-blue waters of the Marshalls in the last days of the year and into the dawn of a new year, 1884.

Suddenly, at 9:30 p.m. on the second day of January, 1884, *Rainier*'s two watchmen cried out, "Breakers ahead!" The captain, just coming on deck, shouted "Hard a-starboard!" But it was too late. *Rainier*'s bow crashed solidly on a partly submerged coral reef ten miles north of the island of Ujae, near a tiny islet, Ebbetyu. Within minutes, the ship was rising and falling back onto the reef, breaking up in the waves with a terrible splintering sound. Much of its stores, food, provisions, and furniture spilled out into the sea within minutes.

All twenty-eight of those on board, the captain, his first mate, the first mate's wife (who was the captain's daughter) and twenty-five other members struggled to save themselves as relentless surf continued to strike the ship in the dark of night.

The *Rainier*'s company had no idea what to expect. Remote as the islands were, the officers knew there was significant trading going on between many islands in the region, mainly in copra, the fruit of the plentiful coconut trees. Yet, there also had been reports of cannibalism in some of these South Sea islands.

The officers and crew spent a miserable and anxious night—working as swiftly as they could in the pounding surf to move perishable goods to the bow of the ship, still holding together better than the stern, while worrying about what the morning would bring.

They weren't exactly sure where they were—except somewhere in the Marshall Islands, in the vast expanse of the Pacific Ocean, a body of water of sixty-four million square miles that could contain all the continents of the world.[1]

Two sailors died in the immediate aftermath of the wreck, one from a lingering illness, the other from exposure. Yet, by early May 1884, four months later, all other members of *Rainier*'s original company were safely on their way back to San Francisco—except for the one person most responsible for their survival and rescue. He remained stranded on Ujae, almost forgotten.

Ironically, that seaman, Will Jackson, was the youngest, lowest paid, and least experienced member of the crew when it left Bath, Maine, in July 1883 to take seventy-three thousand cases of kerosene to Kobe, Japan. Now he wandered the palm tree–dotted beach of the remote atoll for weeks, alone among a small group of elderly natives who spoke a language he could not understand, and lived on a diet of coconuts and breadfruit. An inveterate reader, he had nothing with which to amuse himself but an old almanac and a couple of cans of tobacco.

He had done everything possible to keep all twenty-eight members of *Rainier* alive after the accident. Having risen from ordinary seaman to steward during the four-month voyage prior to the shipwreck, he had commanded a small schooner built from the wreckage to take *Rainier*'s failing captain three hundred miles to a known trading outpost for medical treatment. Then, sailing alone and fighting off an unruly group of natives, he had rushed back to rescue the first mate, the captain's daughter and other seamen, only to find they had been taken off Ujae by an American warship just a day or two before he returned—leaving him stranded once again.

Based in part on a captivating diary and letters home, this is the story of that brave and resourceful young sailor, Richard Willis (Will) Jackson—and how with courage, wit, and resolve, he not only survived the shipwreck and extended periods of isolation in the remote Pacific, but went on to have a more remarkable career in the maritime world than the rest of his shipmates, including a disgraced captain and his unlucky first mate—both of whom had lost two ships within a year.

It is the story of one bold exploit and narrow escape after another from his teenage years to travels around the world, from the Atlantic to the Pacific, down the coast of California to Mexico and beyond, to the whaling and salmon grounds of Alaska and the lumber mills of the northwest. It is the story of a curious, spirited, and ambitious young man who, impelled to go to sea after the bankruptcy of his grandfather's successful shipyard, rose steadily through the ranks of the maritime world to the threshold of captaincy of his own ship.

And it is the story of how blind fate can interfere, in the oddest and most improbable of ways, with the most heroic of lives and adventures.

## Chapter Two

# City of Ships

A FIVE-MINUTE WALK FROM WHERE THE LONG, WINDING KENNEBEC River straightens out in Bath, Maine, the "City of Ships," Andrew Jackson and Harriet Crooker Jackson were expecting their third child in late July 1861. They had a son, Frank, then seven, and a daughter Clara, three—both with the same May 10 birthday.

Richard Willis Jackson, or Will as he would be known, was born on July 31, a week dominated as most days were then by developments in the Civil War. The war that began in April with the Confederate attack on Fort Sumter was now in its fourth month and had seen its first major battle just ten days earlier, at Bull Run, in Virginia (also known as First Manassas).

Union forces had succeeded in driving back Confederate troops at first in a plan to attack Richmond, the Confederate capital. But the largely inexperienced volunteer army was forced to retreat to Washington by rebel reinforcements. It was during that battle that Confederate general Thomas Jonathan Jackson earned the nickname "Stonewall" for his fierce leadership of resistance to the Union attack.

Major appointments of soon-to-be-famous leaders came that week. President Lincoln named General George McClellan as commander of the Union army on July 26; Ulysses S. Grant, William Tecumseh Sherman, and Joseph Hooker were promoted to brigadier general on the day Will Jackson was born.

The Jackson and Crooker families played an active role in the Union cause. Maine, in fact, contributed more soldiers and sailors than any other state on a per capita basis, 73,000. Andrew Jackson, a captain in Bath's militia, drew a deferment for a hernia, but served as an "enrolling officer" in two city wards.

A younger brother of Andrew's wife, Harriet, served on a Union transport ship. Her first cousin, William Frederick Crooker, a private in the Third Maine Infantry, fought at Bull Run, Chancellorsville, and Gettysburg, three of the bloodiest battles of the war, and was wounded twice. He once wrote home that there were "too many balls [bullets] flying around for me."[1]

Andrew and Harriet were living in her father's expansive home in Bath at the time, helping William Donnell Crooker maintain a semblance of authority and connection with four younger children of his, now in their teens and early twenties. Overwhelmed by debts and the panic of 1857, Crooker had been in and out of "confinement" between 1858 and 1863 after being financially devastated by a series of debts, swindles, family tensions, and the Panic of 1857. William and his brother, Charles, had been among the most prominent shipbuilders in Bath and Maine (and, in effect, the entire country) until deep distrust, bad investments, and a series of large land purchases had brought an end to their partnership in 1854.

Andrew, a lawyer by training, an auctioneer, and a merchant, later described as "one of the old landmarks of Bath" for his active engagement in the city's political and cultural life, had been trying to help his father-in-law recover from his misfortune.

With little income themselves, and the mortgage to their father's twenty-room mansion held by a close relative, Andrew and Harriet Jackson were doing their best to manage an extended family of William's children, and now three young children of their own.

It was a tough time. The 1860s and the war brought about deep change to Bath's economic and social life, including a sharp decline in shipbuilding. While Bath and Maine strongly supported the Union, its extensive shipping ties with the South, mainly the triangular trade that carried lumber south, cotton to Europe, and immigrants back across the Atlantic, caused conflicting loyalties, even within leading families. Dozens of Bath ships were in Southern ports in early years of the war.

"Bath and New Orleans were closer neighbors than Washington and Richmond," noted one historian.

———❦———

Two more children came along soon to Andrew and Harriet: Charles, in 1863, and Alice, in 1867. By then, William Donnell Crooker had returned from his last stay behind bars, started a small business, and was reestablishing himself in the community when he died in 1868.

While their parents struggled, Will Jackson and his siblings most likely enjoyed a normal childhood. Their massive home was surrounded by vegetable gardens, fields with livestock, and deep woods on a narrow but miles-long strip of land that had been owned by the Crooker family since the middle of the eighteenth century, when Isaiah Crooker became one of the first twelve settlers of Bath, formerly known as Long Reach. The Crooker house, built by William in 1846–47 at the height of his shipbuilding success, rose high on a bluff that looked down over the Kennebec River and its sprawling shipyards.

The Jackson children had to do little more than roll down the hill to their elementary school in Bath—South Grammar, a block away below their home. Bath was an early advocate of public schooling in Maine; South Grammar and North Grammar schools were built in 1849 at a cost of five thousand dollars each.

Will's boyhood was not especially unusual, though it was marked by several exploits that reflected a daring streak and previsioned an adventurous life.

He was a standout athlete, excelling in several sports, including baseball. He loved a challenge and was said to be fearless. Once while swimming off a wharf on the Kennebec River, he saw a small boat drifting along the opposite shore—a good thirty-minute swim away. He swam to the boat, but as soon as he climbed in, the vessel, leaking badly, sank to the bottom, leaving Will little choice but to swim back to the Bath side of the river.

On another occasion, in his early teens, he rescued a younger boy who fell through thin ice on a small pond. At seventeen, in March 1879, he was struck by lightning and fell unconscious for several hours. He lost use of his limbs briefly, but recovered in a few days. The *Portland Daily Press* reported on April 2, 1879: "Master Will Jackson was able to walk with a cane today. Since the accident Saturday, he has been unable to use his limbs."

Will Jackson's love for adventure and his physical strength were well known in Bath. His derring-do was demonstrated one warm summer's day in 1875 when Will, then fourteen, convinced his younger brother Charles, all of twelve, that they should take their fourteen-foot rowboat and visit a friend in Damariscotta.

A slight obstacle presented itself. Damariscotta, a town approximately twenty miles down east from Bath by road, was close to double that by the Sasanoa River, into Hockomock Bay, through a treacherous spot called Lower Hell's Gate, across the Sheepscot River, to Boothbay Harbor, then around Ocean Point and up the Damariscotta River.

Setting out at 7:00 a.m. with two friends they agreed to drop off in Boothbay Harbor, they rowed for ten hours. A later account of the trip described a daunting voyage, including a short period in the Atlantic Ocean after lunch in Boothbay. By miscalculation, they ended up rowing against the tide in the Damariscotta River.

"People on the shore were beginning to wonder what the light boat was doing, a gunshot from shore, riding along on the crest of ten- to twelve-foot swells and dropping from sight every once in a while. Nearby vessels were showing just the tops of their masts." Not surprisingly, the boys stayed in Damariscotta for two weeks before returning home.[2]

A Bath newspaper portrayed the trip "as a fine illustration of what constituted a day's sport when horses and bicycles were the only vehicles of transportation on shore and trim little rowboats and trimmer sail boats constituted a day's fun on the water."

Based on limited records, Will Jackson was a good student. Bath City reports (1879–1880) list Richard Willis Jackson as a graduate of Bath High School in 1879.

Land for the very first school in Bath was donated by Jackson's great-great grandfather, Isaiah Crooker, who first came to Long Reach

(Bath) in 1748. Both Will's grandfather, William Donnell Crooker, and his brother Charles, attended the Erudition School, built in 1794. Not satisfied with offering just an elementary school education, city fathers established the Bath Academy in 1805. The trustees, including a Crooker, then turned over that academy to the city as a high school in 1852. Bath High School formally began operation in 1860.

The city's high school records describe spartan conditions: one large room for boys, one large room for girls; no running water until 1886; outside toilets. A man who became a judge said students attended classes every day of the week except Sunday. The principal, a Mr. Cole, "was a very stern man and used a two-foot ruler for discipline." Not surprisingly for that period, a course for college-bound students was for boys only.

Richard Willis Jackson was among thirteen seniors who graduated in 1879 in the "first class" of four groups listed. His sisters graduated from Bath High School as well, with honors: Clara, the year before, with a senior thesis titled "Night Brings Out the Stars," and Alice, in 1884, with an essay titled "Pleasures of the Imagination." There is no mention of Charles; Frank, the eldest of five, had died of consumption (the common name then for tuberculosis) in April 1872 at seventeen.

## CHAPTER THREE

# "I Wondered Where the Captain Was?"

*I must go down to the seas again, to the lonely sea and the sky; And all
I ask is a tall ship and a star to steer her by.*

JOHN MASEFIELD'S EVOCATIVE POEM "SEA FEVER" WAS NOT WRITTEN
until 1902, but it accurately describes the attitude of many young men
in New England—especially Maine—who naturally turned to the sea to
make a living in the nineteenth century.

Will Jackson was no different from thousands of other Maine
teenagers and young adults when he decided to cast his fate to going
"before the mast" at the age of twenty or twenty-one. With his father
still struggling to hold onto the Crooker mansion, with the economy in
Bath and Maine only then recovering from a prolonged downturn, Will
signed on to serve as a seaman on the new steam schooner *Jeanie* in 1883
after holding down a series of low-paying jobs in Bath, Bangor, and other
Maine cities and towns following graduation from high school.

Maine sailors, and New Englanders in general, had an edge on young
men from other parts of the United States and increasingly large cohorts
of immigrants in part because they grew up on the Atlantic coast, in towns
where shipbuilding and maritime trade comprised a major industry.

"Up until the middle of the nineteenth century," observed historian
Timothy Lynch, "the sons of the best families went to sea before the mast
with a view to learning the ropes and moving to the quarter-deck, leading
to a pool of professional seamen."[1]

In fact, well into the late 1900s, Maine sailors enjoyed an advantage because of their experience at a younger age. Maine and New England youth often went to sea as early as the age of twelve or fifteen, and, if they survived, their rough-and-tumble initiation stood them in good stead in ports around the United States and the globe.

Their experience—plus networks of friends and acquaintances from home—enabled many to avoid falling victim to harsh treatment, especially the scurrilous practice of "crimping." Many shipowners and sea captains employed ruthless agents, or "crimps," often boardinghouse managers and workers, to assemble a crew for their next voyage. The crimps basically bribed incoming sailors soon after their ship docked, getting them drunk and offering them advance funds for a new shipboard assignment. Crimps pocketed as much as 25 percent of a victim's wages. The practice was common around the world, and especially in the port of San Francisco—a port Will Jackson would come to know well.

The British consul in San Francisco, a Mr. Booker, sent this report to the Foreign Office in London in 1872 about a practice he said was carried on there "to a disgraceful extent."

> *Vessels of all nations are boarded by numbers of boarding-house "runners" before the anchor is down, and in times when Seamen are scarce the sailors are almost dragged from the ship, taken to the various houses [bars and brothels], and after a few days of dissipation, the victims are shipped [to sea] with two or three months' advance wages.*[2]

Before they came to, the unfortunate seamen often were on board a vessel, well out to sea on a long and rigorous voyage—with little recourse or rights.

—◦—

While his grandfather William Donnell Crooker had been a shipbuilder and not a sea captain, several of Will Jackson's relatives and friends had gone to sea at an early age and earned their mate's license or captain's papers.

One of the most noteworthy—and notorious—was Charles Crooker Duncan, a first cousin of William Donnell Crooker, and later the New York broker for William and his brother Charles at the height of their shipbuilding success (1845–54). Duncan, growing up in Bath, started out as a cabin boy at sixteen on the Crookers' *Glasgow*, a full-rigged ship built for them in 1837 by the famed shipwright Johnson Rideout.

Overcoming forty-eight hours of seasickness from rolling seas on that first trip, Duncan went on to become a first mate and then captain of another Crooker ship, *Swanton*, at age twenty-three. As *Swanton* sailed from Boston to Charleston, SC, on a bright winter day in 1844, Duncan later recalled that "the ship was well past Cape Cod before I could shed the habit of wondering where the captain was."[3]

———

Voyages such as *Swanton*'s from Bath to Charleston and New Orleans were a vital part of the "coastal" trade and later the "triangular" trade in which Maine-built vessels played a dominant role. The coastal trade, predominantly in the 1820s and '30s, featured schooners and brigs that carried agricultural goods and lumber to the southern US and Caribbean islands, returning with staples ranging from fruit, sugar, and molasses to coffee and rum.

Starting in the mid-1830s, ever-larger vessels—full-rigged ships— took the same products south, but then loaded bales of cotton for European ports such as Liverpool and Le Havre, now centers of the Industrial Revolution. The ships then completed the triangle, bringing back across the Atlantic large numbers of immigrants from all over Europe, a trend accelerated by political and economic turmoil there.

The United States in the middle part of the nineteenth century was an appealing destination for all kinds of people. It remained that way into the end of the century and the early twentieth century. With its steady growth, free-wheeling politics, and open spaces, the New World continued to attract millions. By 1880, the population of the country had increased to fifty million, approximately 6.6 million of whom were foreign-born.

A tidal wave of immigration led to widespread unrest throughout the country in much of the nineteenth century. Nativism, the fear of native-born American loss of jobs, status, and political influence, led to demonstrations and riots in different cities as far back as 1834, when there was anti-Catholic rioting in Charlestown, Massachusetts, and Bangor, Maine.

The rise of the secretive Know-Nothing party in the 1840s and '50s stemmed from a strong undercurrent of nativism after the arrival of nearly two million Catholics escaping the Great Hunger in Ireland after 1845. Know-Nothing mobs burned down the South Church in Bath in July 1854 during riots against Irish and German Catholics.[4]

The flood of immigrants continued, however, attracted by the spread of industrialization across the United States—a transformation accelerated by completion of a national rail network. The painful, violence-ridden aftermath of the Civil War during Reconstruction and brutal removal and marginalization of Native American tribes did not slow the rapid growth of the Midwest and Far West. Cities grew by leaps and bounds as factories, steel mills, and other mass production businesses developed along the expansion of rail lines across the continent. Not even appalling financial scandals—led by railroad corruption—and hapless political leadership slowed that momentum for long.[5]

Waves of Chinese immigrants arrived on the West Coast from the 1850s to the 1880s, leading to passage of the Chinese Exclusion Act by Congress in 1882. The law, the first significant anti-immigration measure, was designed to placate citizens who felt the Chinese were to blame for low wages and economic difficulties—even though Chinese accounted for just .002 percent of the nation's populace.

Corporate formation led to financial giants such as John D. Rockefeller's Standard Oil Company, established in 1882 and soon dominating the energy industry of that period and for decades to come. Thomas A. Edison's invention of the electric light bulb on October 22, 1879, brought about an eventual decline in the use of kerosene as an illuminant.

Alexander Graham Bell had invented the telephone in 1876. And in Rochester, New York, George Eastman gained a patent on a flexible roll of film that revolutionized photography.

The ninth decade of the nineteenth century opened with political turmoil. James A. Garfield, an intellectually gifted Ohio farmer and Civil War general, defeated both the favorite, former president Ulysses S. Grant, and the Speaker of the House, Maine's James G. Blaine, for the Republican party nomination. He then bested the Democratic nominee, Winfield Scott Hancock, a Union army hero, in the 1880 presidential election.

Less than four months after his inauguration in March 1881, Garfield was shot by an unhinged religious fanatic as he was about to board a train in the capital. He survived for two and one-half months, and died only after archaic and unsanitary medical treatment by his doctors. Using new technology, an "induction balance," Alexander Graham Bell, a close friend of Garfield's, made a valiant effort to find the fatal bullet—unsuccessful due to the meddling of Garfield's doctor.[6]

New technology also played a role in the first ship on which Will Jackson went to sea. The steam schooner *Jeanie,* an 800-ton, 186-foot vessel, was built in Bath in the winter of 1882–83 by Goss, Sawyer, and Packard, now the largest yard in the city.

*Jeanie* made a few trips to the Caribbean, but was built to be employed as a supply vessel for whaling and Alaskan salmon ships in the western Arctic, where it was in service for many years. More correctly called a "steam auxiliary schooner," it was one of only two such vessels built in Maine.

Carrying anywhere from one to four masts, they were cheaper to build, required less crew, and had far more space for bulk commodities such as lumber and coal, which it also needed to burn. In addition to providing power if winds slackened, the engines were used to load cargo, raise sails, and hoist anchors into place.

*Jeanie,* owned by a J. Winchester, passed its early trials in late February and March of 1883 with flying colors. A long account in the *Bath Daily Times* reported that it steamed a total of fifteen miles from Bath down the Kennebec River to Parker's Head and back in one hour and 29 minutes with "speed, ease of working and general sailing points admirably displayed and satisfactory."

The paper described the vessel's "machinery," including two engines, one of high pressure, the other low pressure, both with a reversing link similar to a locomotive. "It consists of an endless screw that [is] turned by a crank and operates a system of geering [sic] and chains that lifts the stack or lowers it at will." The vessel is also "richly furnished and elaborately appointed in the best style; one of the finest crafts that ever laid at the wharf in this city."[7]

The March 1 trial narrowly avoided a disaster when the chief engineer of *Jeanie* was hit by an errant pin that came loose and struck him "like a shot" in the knee. No bones were broken, the newspaper reported, "but it was a narrow escape from a fatal accident."

---

Visiting friends, fun and games, and hard work characterized one of three trips Will Jackson made aboard *Jeanie* in the spring and early summer of 1883—the third to Baltimore, Havana, and Trinidad.

The owner, Mr. Winchester, accompanied the ship on its maiden voyage to check out operation of his new vessel. Will reported to his father that Mr. Winchester decided to do away with the top masts and jib boom—"as we steam all the time." The ship would retain four "strip masts," so "she will be a beauty."

"Will Jackson of this city is on the steamer *Jeanie* which runs from New York to Havana," the *Bath Times* reported in its "Local News" column on May 9.

The widespread presence of Bath ships and seamen, both officers and crew members from Bath and the mid-coast region, was reflected in Will's letters home. In Baltimore, he visited with two friends, Jack Patten and Will Sewall, the latter one of two sons of his mother's cousin Emma Crooker Sewall. Both were in school there, Will (Sewall) at Johns Hopkins University. He went to a baseball "match." Two Bath-built ships were tied up in Baltimore, *Louisiana* and *George B. Adams*. Another, *B. W. Morse*, named for a major Bath shipbuilder, was docked in Havana. Will went on board to talk to the captain, Greer Hawley, and the steward, both friends from Bath.

The trip from Baltimore to Havana took seven days, without incident. After a few days, *Jeanie* sailed—or steamed—to Sangre de Grande, Trinidad, to take on a load of sugar before returning to New York. The owner, according to Will, planned to have some further repairs made in New York, so "I shall run down home" by mid-June.

He promised to bring a box of Cuban cigars home to his younger brother, Charles, and fruit, bananas and oranges, for the ladies at home "if I can get any that will keep." Leaving Baltimore for Havana, he sent a postcard to his father, Andrew. "We go in the stream in about an hour, so I won't be able to write till I get to Havana. Give love to all, and good luck till you hear from me. Your son, Will."

Will did return to Bath in mid-June. The *Bath Times* highlighted his arrival in its "Local News" column. "Will Jackson—on the schooner *Jeanie*—returned by the Boston boat this morning. He reports the *Jeanie* as a fine sailer." The schooner, he told the newspaper, made a speedy return from Cuba to New York in four days, at one point covering 530 miles in 30 hours.

Jackson did not stay long. The Sewall shipyard was completing another large vessel, *Rainier,* reportedly chartered for Japan, and Will found a way to sign on as a seaman within one week after his return.

He did bring cigars home to his brother Charles, now graduated from high school, but completely happy in his home town, and showing little interest in his brother's search for adventure.

Two years behind Will leaving high school, Charles had gone to work in Fogg's store in Bath. Despite long hours according to his diary in 1880 and 1881, he maintained a busy social life, regularly going ice skating, taking in the Topsham Fair or a visiting circus, attending various church and other social events—returning virtually every evening with a Kate D., or a Miss Ashworth, or another young lady. He played baseball and pool. The proud owner of his own sailboat, he devoted Sundays to repairs during the winter and trips with friends down the Kennebec River and around coastal islands in spring and summer.

On July 31, 1881, Will's twentieth birthday, Charles was more interested in the fact he had "carried passengers out to the USS *Saratoga* (a visiting warship), and earned six dollars."[8]

CHAPTER FOUR

# "The Large Vessel"—*Rainier*

SHIPBUILDING IN MAINE AND ALONG THE EASTERN SEABOARD DECLINED sharply in the years following the Civil War. It was the beginning of a dark age for the American merchant marine.

Damage by Confederate raiders during the war, tough regulations imposed by Great Britain, and high insurance costs reduced both shipbuilding and trade by huge percentages. During the war years, the percentage of exports and imports carried in American ships fell from 65.2 in 1861 to 27.7 in 1865, recovering slightly after the war.

Maine's governor Sidney Perham began his inaugural message in 1871 by saying "how humiliating it was to see the business carried on under the American flag monopolized by and bearing the flag of the nation [Britain] that contributed the most in our time of trouble to sweep our commerce from the ocean."

Most of the vessels now built in Maine and nearby states tended to be schooners, designed mainly for fishing interests and a more coastal trade carrying coal and lumber.

Yet within a few years, shipbuilding began to recover. Nearly twenty shipyards were in operation in Bath alone, producing both full-rigged ships and ever-larger schooners. "The shipyards were busier than at any time since 1863-1864 and vessels were built and thrown into the sea with facility and dispatch unknown in former years."[1]

Throughout these years, one yard remained a steady producer of both ships and jobs in shipbuilding. The E. & A. Sewall Company dated back to the 1820s, when William D. Sewall first took shares in or was the registered owner of several vessels, including a brig *Diana*, a brig *Lewis*, and a ninety-nine-ton schooner, *Emulous*.

The company was known as Clark and Sewall for decades, and then in 1854 became E. & A. Sewall, now managed by the two surviving sons of William D.—Edward and Arthur.

Building on a regular production of at least one ship a year by Clark and Sewall, E. & A. Sewall and then Arthur Sewall & Company often averaged two a year from soon after its new incorporation in 1854.

In 1854, the year termed "the golden period of shipbuilding in Bath," Bath, Maine, built more ships in terms of tonnage than all but two other cities in the United States—more than Philadelphia, Baltimore, or other major shipbuilding locales. Only Boston and New York built more, and many of New York's vessels that year were canal boats. The Sewall firm was one of the most consistent builders for decades to come.[2]

A Sewall carpenter, Henry Merryman, recalled: "There were many yards. As soon as one ship was launched the keel of another was placed. No one ever thought that the business would ever die."[3]

Arthur Sewall seemed destined to become the scion of the Sewall family. He was the youngest of four sons and two daughters of William D. and Rachel Trufant Sewall. The eldest son became a minister, the second was killed in a fatal accident in the Clark & Sewall yard in 1851, and Edward, who had a serious problem with alcoholism, died in 1879 after falling from a balcony in a New York hotel.

—⁓—

Will Jackson may well have spent a fair bit of time in the Sewall shipyard in the 1870s—if mainly as a visitor. Emma Duncan Crooker, the eldest daughter of Will's grandfather's brother, Charles Crooker, had married Arthur Sewall in March 1859. Their two sons, Harold and William, were born in 1860 and 1861—the latter the same year as Will Jackson. The younger Sewall son was also called Will. They attended the same high school in Bath.

The Crooker brothers' shipyard, one of the most prominent in Maine in the middle of the nineteenth century, and for a few short years just as productive as the Sewall yard, had folded in 1854 after prolonged distrust and severe financial setbacks. But while Will's grandfather, William Donnell Crooker, continued building ships for a few years, fighting the firm's debts and being incarcerated on three occasions, his brother Charles remained free of trouble. Charles Crooker withdrew from active shipbuilding, but invested in several ships built in Maine in the 1850s and 1860s, including two Sewall ships, *Thrasher* and *El Capitan*. He also lent substantial sums of money from time to time to his son-in-law, Arthur.

The resurgence of shipbuilding in the 1870s was in large part due to a substantial increase in schooners rather than full-rigged ships. Though they were larger than earlier schooners, the newer vessels could be built in less time, leading to some increase in unemployment. Of the 353 vessels built in Bath between 1871 and 1880, 195 were schooners averaging 269 tons. Yet, one hundred and fifteen full-rigged ships, among them the "Downeasters" known for their full sails and extensive space for large cargoes, were built in the same period. Shipbuilding in Bath and Maine surged despite the devastating national effects of the financial panic of 1873.

While steel-hulled ships were beginning to be the focus of shipbuilding, especially in Britain, by 1882 "Bath was turning out a greater number of wooden vessels every year than any other place in the world," observed historian William Avery Baker. Approximately six thousand men were employed in ship-related jobs in Bath—on land and at sea. In 1882 alone, Bath launched more than seventy vessels.

The principal shipbuilders remained pretty much the same group as it had been for thirty-five years, with an overall value estimated at four million dollars in 1877.

The Patten yard, once proud owners of the largest Bath-based fleet, was sold to the Sewall company in 1872. And there was one significant newcomer, Goss and Sawyer.[4]

In the next two-and-a-half decades, Goss and Sawyer, followed by Goss, Sawyer, and Packard, and eventually the New England Shipbuilding Company, became the dominant shipyard in Bath, responsible for production of more than one hundred ships in a twenty-year span, mostly schooners.

Despite political strife in the late 1870s and 1880s, the city of Bath experienced considerable progress with an expanding diversity in its economic base, numerous public improvements, and a vibrant cultural life.

While shipbuilding continued to be a major employer, manufacturing in several areas, highlighted by the existence of thirty steam engines, was turning out many different commodities. The boom in the ice trade continued. A new public water supply system was developed, and electric lighting replaced the dim gaslights. The Patten family deeded property to establish the city's library, and the Sagadahoc Historical Society was formed.

City leaders also recognized that the age of sail was coming to an end. City officials and shipbuilders together established a Manufacturing Commission, which led to production of marine engines and steel-hulled vessels. In 1882, Thomas W. Hyde, a former Union army general and mayor of Bath, organized the Hyde Windlass Company to help power new ships. His company soon became the Bath Iron Works, today one of the world's leading shipyards.[5]

Along with the Houghton and Rogers yards, the Sewall shipyard remained one of the few older shipbuilding entities in the city of ships in the 1880s, despite the death of Edward Sewall in 1879.

The company, now titled Arthur Sewall & Company, built three vessels in 1881, a ship and two schooners, and four in 1882—two ships, including a well-known Downeaster, *W. F. Babcock*, and two schooners.

In 1883, the firm built a 159.5-foot-long schooner, *Blanche Allen*, and then constructed its only full-rigged ship that year, *Rainier*. Local papers offered frequent reports of "the large vessel" being built in the Sewall yard during 1883—a sure sign that its owners were still mulling over its name right up to its launch.

A few days before its launch, the *Bath Times* merely reported "The ship at A. Sewall and Co. will be coppered on the stocks. The yellow material arrived yesterday."

What was all the hoopla about anyway? Ships were being launched all the time in Bath. Far more exciting was the imminent arrival of Forepaugh's Circus, a celebrated touring ensemble featuring elephants, camels, and a high-flying trapeze act. Parades and brass bands were set up to welcome and serenade the circus under a huge tent that could hold up to ten thousand.

On June 23, 1883, a Saturday, the *Bath Daily Times* devoted a brief article to formal completion of the new ship—headlined "Launch." Revealing the name *Rainier* for the first time, the paper gave little more information than its dimensions, and concluded: "It is not yet decided who is to command her. She is owned by the builders and other parties in the city."

Assigned the official registry number of 110586 by US Customs, *Rainier*'s dimensions were 1,877 tons, 233 feet in length, 42 feet in breadth, and 18 feet in depth. It was described as having a stem head and an elliptical stern. It was very similar to *W.F. Babcock*, built the year before.

The provenance of its name is not certain, but expert sources attribute it to the Sewall family's travels and admiration for mountains, especially in the American West. In his book *Live Yankees*, William H. Bunting explained the origin of the naming of the Sewalls' 1,493-ton *El Capitan*, in 1873. "Her name was suggested by William D. [Arthur Sewall's father] after a trip to Yosemite where he had seen and admired the spectacular monolith of that name."

Mt. Rainier in the state of Washington had been named for a British naval officer, Rear Admiral Peter Rainier, in 1792. It had been called "Tahoma" by native Northwestern Americans.

Samuel H. Morrison, an experienced master who had recently lost a Sewall ship, *Oracle*, was named captain. Omar J. Humphrey, Morrison's first mate on *Oracle*, the ship lost off Cape Horn earlier in 1883, was named first mate again. Humphrey had just married Emma Morrison, the captain's daughter, and she was to accompany her new husband and father on *Rainier*'s maiden voyage. Will Jackson, now twenty-one, was one of the crew, a motley group of American, Scandinavian, Italian, and

Russian seamen. He was the youngest member of the crew, and lowest paid at twelve dollars a month.[6]

*Rainier* would sail in ballast to Philadelphia where it would load its cargo: seventy-three thousand containers of case oil or kerosene, shipped in hundreds of wooden crates containing two five-gallon tins each.

Due to plenty of space and less need for a large crew, square-rigged Downeasters like *Rainier* were popular ships to take kerosene on the long trip around Cape Horn to Asia and Oceania in the latter part of the nineteenth century, especially for Rockefeller's Standard Oil Company. By the end of the century, California produced a quarter of the world's "illuminating oil," or kerosene, considered safe, clean, and effective, and that lucrative shipping trade was a precursor to the export of petroleum.[7]

Though the invention took decades to spread in even advanced countries, Thomas Alva Edison's invention of the electric light bulb on October 22, 1879, in Menlo Park, New Jersey, eventually took its toll on the kerosene trade.

———

*Rainier* departed Bath on July 7, 1883, following final touches and key steps, including insurance and completion of a charter party for the ship to carry the large cargo of kerosene from Philadelphia to Hiogo (Kobe), Japan.

Salter and Livermore, the company handling the cargo on the American end, with the China and Japan Trading Company in the Far East, wrote to Arthur Sewall that the shipment would be the largest ever loaded for Japan on a sailing vessel, and only exceeded by one steamer.

One of the very last orders of supplies was clearly meant for the crew to celebrate their departure or arrival in Philadelphia. In addition to forty-eight barrels of beef, twenty-four barrels of pork, five hundred pounds of codfish and twelve hundred pounds of bread, the manifest included four cases of lobsters, totaling $19.20, and four cases of clams, provisioned by the Portland Packing Company shortly before *Rainier* sailed. The company apologized for not being able to find "pie peaches" in Portland. *Rainier* did carry one other unusual item: a piano, a wedding present from Captain and Mrs. Morrison to their daughter, Emma.

*Rainier's* departure was well covered in the local newspapers of the day. The *Bath Daily Times* carried reports from both Bath and Parker's Head, a small village halfway down the Kennebec River to the Atlantic Ocean. "The new ship *Rainier*," the paper noted, "made a beautiful appearance as she passed out to sea yesterday. Her colors were visible above the highest land of the Head."

## CHAPTER FIVE

# Knocked in the Head

ONCE FREE OF THE KENNEBEC RIVER FROM BATH, A TRICKY, TWELVE-mile run undertaken only with the tide running out, *Rainier* flew south around Cape Cod and down the East Coast to Philadelphia in five days.

Captain Morrison reported to Arthur Sewall that the new ship "works well, and reached 11 and 1/2 knots best speed on its maiden voyage. Have good crew."

Going up the Delaware River in mid-July 1883, the ship docked, discharged its ballast, and began loading its cargo without delay. Approximately 2,400 cases of kerosene were loaded in the first day as a test trial. The rest of the 73,000 cases would have to be loaded "in the stream" so other ships could tie up and discharge.

The *Rainier*'s destination of Hiogo (Kobe), Japan, was all charted, roughly—down the Atlantic, around the tip of southern Africa (Cape of Good Hope), through the Indian Ocean, into the Tasman Sea, around southern Australia and New Zealand and north to Japan. The distance in the nineteenth century—from Bath—was roughly 16,700 nautical miles.[1]

Meanwhile, the loading of the cargo would take a good while. Enough to allow both Captain Morrison, his daughter, and first mate Omar Humphrey to return home to Bath for their wedding. Crew members were given shore leave. The second mate, Harry Whalen Drohan, and Will Jackson, remained in charge. (Jackson always referred to him as Whalen.)

Will wrote home that "you would laugh to see us getting our own meals, [but] I like it better than the grub the cook gave us. He was not much of a cook."

The two men whiled away their time, overseeing the loading but also taking excursions ashore—to the large department store, Wanamaker's, to dinners with Bath friends, and rowing upriver to see mates from Maine on other ships.

It was on return from one of the latter trips, two weeks after their arrival in Philadelphia, four days before they were to sail for Japan, that Will and two colleagues found their plans were "knocked in the head." They were rowing to the *Rainier* on a Sunday evening when they "heard a crash, and looked toward the vessel and saw her sinking." An English steamer, *Sherbourne,* from Huelva, Spain, had struck *Rainier* on its side, driving the latter's anchor through its own starboard side, and immobilizing both ships. "I tell you my heart came up in my mouth when I heard the crash," Will wrote to his father on July 31, 1883 (his twenty-second birthday). "Will probably be here some time yet for repairs."

The *Bath Daily Times* carried an article on the accident on August 2. "A Philadelphia dispatch states that Tuesday night, Steamer *Sherbourne* collided off League Island with ship *Rainier* for Yokohama. Both vessels were considerably damaged."

Captain Morrison dutifully reported the accident to Arthur Sewall. "We were lying in a lawful position, with signal light burning brightly when the *Sherbourne* came up the river full speed."

Barely a week later, however, *Rainier* was repaired and ready for sea. The total cost of repairs of thirteen planks, replacement of its jib boom and an anchor, $5,820, was paid in full by insurers of the English vessel. Some last-minute acquisitions in Philadelphia included seventy live chickens and twelve (Sharp and Springfield) rifles.

The *Rainier*'s total company numbered twenty-eight, including Morrison's daughter, Emma. Six sailors who had left Bath failed to report in Philadelphia, but others took their places. The "Articles of Agreement between Master and Seamen in the Merchant Service of the United States" stipulated that the voyage would last eighteen months, that no wages would be paid until its completion, that liberty to go ashore could be granted only by the master, and that no sheath knives nor liquor nor "profane language" would be allowed on board.

Will wrote a long letter to his father, Andrew, older sister Clara, now married and mother of a baby, younger sister Alice, and his brother Charles, just before the ship's departure. He also sent his best wishes to "Annie," his father's new (second) wife. Andrew Jackson and Mrs. Annie L. Jones, of Thomaston, were married May 12, 1883—an event Will had missed because he was on board *Jeanie* in the Caribbean. Harriet Crooker Jackson, Andrew's first wife, had died in 1878, age fifty-six.[2]

"I thought I would write a few lines tonight as this is the last chance I shall get to post a letter for some time. The sailors are coming aboard tomorrow, and we shall probably be at sea by tomorrow night."

Will said he was sending his watch and chain home, as well as a ticket for the boat from Boston to Bath that he had not used. He closed the letter with a challenge to his brother Charles to "race you for a Moustache. I shan't shave until we cross the Line [the Equator], then Neptune will come aboard and shave me."

On August 9, *Rainier* "got underway" at 3 a.m. but remained under tow until after breakfast. It finally moved out of the Delaware River later that day and passed Cape May at about 9:00 p.m.

According to Will Jackson's faithfully kept "Diary of the Voyage of the Ship *Rainier* from Phila. To Japan," the ship was "at sea, fresh wind, running S. by S.," and he had the forenoon watch on deck.

He reported (to his diary) that "most of the crew are young fellows; have not learned their names yet; the mate won't allow me to speak to them much; keeps me aft." He spent part of the first afternoon in navigation lessons from the second mate Drohan, and stood watch again from 8:00 p.m. to 12:00 midnight.

*Rainier* initially headed east straight into the Atlantic to avoid the south to north flow of the Gulf Stream. Given the power of the Gulf Stream, a warm, swift ocean current which serves as a large engine for the global climate, sailing ships leaving the east coast had little choice but to hug the shore if going south or move far enough into the ocean to avoid it. Morrison chose the latter, and the voyage proceeded apace, encountering little in the way of major storms or dead calm—at first. A cold, drizzling rain, with southwest winds, prevailed. On August 12, Will reported "wet weather, quite rough, shipping some water over the side, got wet through, put sail on, pumped Ship; after coffee at five, cleared decks, had a supper and went to sleep. Turned out 7 bells, worked and dressed. . . . Then relieved the wheel." After supper, back on deck, he reported that "[I] like first mate, was aloft today for the first time. Mr. Whalen [Drohan] is teaching me Navigation."

Writing more on that day than in most entries on the rest of the trip, he added: "Have been eating watermelon ever since we left. Mr. Percy and I bought a stock before we left. Have a room all to myself, starboard side of Mid Ship, where have plenty of room. Like all the officers. Jammed one finger last Thursday with the fish hook. Getting better. Turn in at 8. All well."

Will recorded that he was "making good progress" in his studies of navigation. "It comes easy to me, and the second mate says I am doing first rate." Within ten days of departure, *Rainier* was well out in the Atlantic Ocean, east of Cape Hatteras, but starting to turn southeast. But Will was still learning: On that tenth day he mistakenly reported that they were about to cross the equator. The equator was still another week or more away.

After rain and squalls for several days, *Rainier* found northeast trade winds, "gentle at first, but in a few days increasing to fresh breezes and lovely weather," according to first mate Omar Humphrey's account in his book *Wreck of the Rainier*. Humphrey noted that such weather allows a hard-working crew to relax, "knowing the wind is steady and that there are no sails to furl and no yards to brace." Soon enough, however, the winds disappeared, and the ship entered the "doldrums, where the sea looks like glass, with a long, undulating motion, which makes the sails slat against the mast as the ship rolls sluggishly in the trough of the sea, and seems to say 'I have sailed my best, I want to rest.'"

Will Jackson's diary entries for the next two weeks were brief, perfunctory. He washed the deck, painted, cleaned brass. He stood watch, usually four hours—reading a book, writing a letter home, taking naps.

Except for a report on the 15th of "whipping gusts all day, makes for slippery work," his diary reported nothing unusual: the longitude and latitude, occasional sighting of another ship, rigging repairs, the weather and his times on and off watch. He did burn his hand one day on fast-moving rope lowering the halyard, but soon felt fine.

———

On Sunday, August 26, Will wrote a brief note in his diary.

"On deck till 8, cleaning Brass. Nothing doing. Squally rain, not much wind, handling sail, pumping. Reading. Got the Lat—34-19N, Long 45 W. On deck, watch below. A Brig in sight to leeward. All well." *Rainier* was in the middle of the Atlantic, still headed southeastward.

On Monday, August 27, Will's notes were pretty much the same. "On duty till 4. Turn in till 8. On deck, squally. Not much out of the usual run. All well."

Roughly eight thousand nautical miles away to the south and east, near dawn Monday, August 27, 1883, four successive explosions off the Indonesian coast threw boulders, congealed lava, and other parts of the landscape fifteen to seventeen miles into the sky, creating immense seawaves and darkening the skies with black smoke and deadly gases. The volcano of Krakatoa had erupted.

In the moment and the immediate aftermath of the eruption, 165 villages on the island of Krakatoa, its archipelago, and the more heavily populated coasts of Java and Sumatra were devastated; 36,417 people died and uncountable thousands were injured. Almost all were victims not of the initial explosion and burning lava but of the huge waves, or tsunamis, that were propelled outward from the volcano.[3]

A Dutch harbor pilot walking on a beach several miles from the volcano, ducking flying rocks and bits of lava, offered a compelling account of a terrifying scene. "Looking out to sea, I noticed a dark black object through the gloom, traveling towards the shore. At first sight, it seemed like a low range of hills rising out of the water—but I knew there was nothing of the kind in the Sunda Strait. A second glance—and a hurried one at that—convinced me that it was a lofty ridge of water many feet high."

The pilot reported watching the bodies of many friends float by moments later as he clung to a palm tree.

The last and largest of the four explosions at 10:02 a.m., August 27, unleashing a wall of water more than one hundred feet high and traveling at speeds of sixty miles per hour, accounted for a large proportion of the deaths.

One of the most thunderous eruptions in history was heard three thousand miles away, and has been estimated to have had an explosive force of two hundred megatons of TNT, approximately ten times that of the atomic bomb dropped on Hiroshima in 1945.

The 2,600-foot-high Krakatoa, or "pointed mountain" as it was known before it virtually disappeared, had begun rumbling in May 1883. Three months later, following smoke and bits of lava flying out of its cone, the four explosions on August 27 darkened the sky worldwide for years and produced spectacular sunsets that inspired many famous artists in their painting of landscapes. Due to geological factors and the open waters of the Indian Ocean, more of the shock waves and sea waves went westward, with less effect eastward in Asia. Vivid red sunsets reportedly triggered alarms and fire engine responses in several cities of the east coast of the United States, including Poughkeepsie, New York, and New Haven, Connecticut. Temperatures around the world remained below normal for five years.[4]

On *Rainier*, reporting Lat. 32-01, Long 44, on August 28, Will Jackson noticed nothing more than "good breeze blowing from the North East . . . throwing some water on deck. All well." A day, two days later, the weather was "squally" with a "fine wind" and the ship was making 9 knots, covering 166 miles in one day.

Other than his navigation lessons, burning his hand, which relieved him of "the wheel" for a week, and the sighting of two brigs in the distance, Jackson's log did show that he also was developing a fine grasp of nautical tasks and details. On September 2, he wrote that in "blowing hard" winds, he had helped take in the higher, lighter sails on *Rainier*, "the skysails, royals, and gallant staysails." Otherwise, his diary kept a straightforward, daily report of squalls or fine weather, latitude and longitude readings, and his sign-off of "All well" into mid-September.

The extended delay in Philadelphia, most of it due to the accident, had been a blessing, or *Rainier* might well have been nearing Krakatoa.

## CHAPTER SIX

# A Splendid Run

BY SUNDAY, SEPTEMBER 9, *RAINIER* CONTINUED TO SAIL SOUTH/SOUTH-east—slowly. There was a lot of rain, not much wind. One month from its departure, *Rainier* was now heading more to the southeast, approximately one thousand miles west of the coast of Senegal in Africa. Jackson wrote that he and the crew hoped to see the Southern Cross, one of the most spectacular constellations in the Southern Hemisphere, "tonight."

The only major development on the ship was the illness of the steward, Frank Silva, and Will Jackson was appointed to replace him, temporarily. A steward had several responsibilities, mainly as the captain's aide for nonsailing activities, such as care of living and eating quarters, and maintaining an inventory of supplies. Will's new role led to several disagreements with the cook, who came under the steward's authority. Will reported "a row with cook" on several days—but that ended up strengthening his place on the ship. After one argument, Captain Morrison reprimanded the cook and sent him packing. "Captain says I suit him, so am all right," Will recorded in his diary.

Despite tough luck, having lost two ships, Captain Samuel Morrison was a mild-mannered, widely respected master. An older brother Parker, like Samuel a native of Phippsburg (near Bath), Maine, had held command of several Sewall ships, including the legendary *Indiana*.[1]

Will Jackson and other members of *Rainier* were very fortunate to have a leader with Morrison's demeanor. And Will had a famous account at hand to make comparisons. He was reading Richard Henry Dana's *Two Years Before the Mast.*

Ship captains in the days of sail were notorious for brutal treatment of crews. Given the dangers of the open ocean and the nature of unruly seamen prone to heavy drink and violent history, strict command and unwavering obedience were necessary. But brutality was not.

As *Rainier* headed southeast in the Atlantic on its long voyage, Jackson was reading several nautical books, including the lively narrative of shipboard life in Dana's book. He offered no comment on the book, but he must have made mental comparisons between Captain Morrison and the master of the brig *Pilgrim*, Francis A. Thompson, under whom Dana had gone to sea in 1836 as an ordinary sailor.

A Mainer himself, Thompson ruled his ship with an iron fist. Though the trip from Boston to California proceeded smoothly, with nary a bad storm or personal incident on board, a series of misunderstandings, slights, and perceived insults, mixed with the tensions built up over closed quarters for so many months, led to a vicious encounter in lower California between the captain and two crew members, both highly respected.

Dana, the well-educated son of a leading New England family who sought adventure while trying to recover from problems with his eyesight, described the build-up to the incident. It came as the ship reached a desolate California port called San Pedro where the crew was put to onerous work, late into the night, up early the next day, loading hides for trade further south.

*Captain Thompson was a vigorous, energetic fellow; he was always active and driving.*

*The length of the voyage, which made us dissatisfied, made the captain feel the necessity of order and strict discipline. Severity created discontent, and signs of discontent provoked severity.*

*Demanding an apology for something a crew member allegedly said, Thompson ordered other crew members to stretch "Sam" out "spread eagle" against the mast.*

*"Will you ever be impudent to me again?"*

*"I never have been," said Sam.*

*"Seize that man up," the captain ordered. "Seize him up. Make a spread eagle of him. I'll teach you all who is master aboard."*

Thompson then proceeded to flog Sam eight to ten times.

*This made me feel sick and almost faint, angry and excited as I was. A man, a human being, fastened up and flogged like a beast. A man, too, whom I had lived with and eaten with for months, and knew almost as well as a brother.*

*The first and almost uncontrollable impulse was resistance, but what was to be done.*

*A second man, a Swedish crew member who had dared to ask the captain what Sam had done, was clapped in irons, then flogged, just as mercilessly.*

Dana concluded his observation on the grim reality of life at sea:

*What is there for sailors to do? If they resist, it is mutiny; and if they succeed, and take the vessel, it is piracy. If a sailor resists his commander, he resists the law, and piracy or submission are his only alternatives. Bad as it was, it must be borne."*[2]

The presence of Captain Morrison's daughter, Emma, on *Rainier*, certainly helped to provide a temperate mood and mitigate potential tensions.

The middle of Samuel and Harriet Morrison's three daughters, Emma was a twenty-one-year-old beauty with striking reddish-gold hair and hazel eyes. An older sister was already an accomplished pianist, which perhaps accounted for her parents' wedding gift of the piano, now placed in the main cabin of *Rainier*.

The presence of a woman on board in days of sail was not unusual. While common superstition in those days had women as bearers of bad luck, companies often allowed wives of captains and senior officers on board. In Emma Morrison Humphrey's case, she had several advantages in her favor: daughter of the master, wife of the first mate, and newly married, so no children. Plus, by all accounts, she was a strong, independent, and talented woman.[3]

Will Jackson struck up a friendly relationship with Emma during the long voyage. They were close in age and may well have attended the same schools in Bath.

According to his diary, Will had frequent conversations with her—especially when he served as steward when the assigned officer, Frank Silva, fell in and out of illness with regularity during the long voyage. At one point, he referred to Emma as "my bookkeeper." He noted that one day while he was on watch, he and Emma had a three-hour "chat." She sometimes served tea to Will and Drohan, the second mate.

———

*Rainier* crossed the equator on Sunday, September 23, 1883. Other than passing several ships, their voyage continued directly south, without trouble.

The ship appeared to be sailing with the northeasterly wind and it was taking them a bit to the southwest now. On September 28, they could see Trinidad Isle, a Brazilian islet almost directly east of Rio de Janeiro.

Two weeks later, October 9, in steady rain and stiff winds, the crew spotted the isle of Tristan da Cunha–the most remote inhabited island on earth. Located 1,511 miles west of Cape Town, South Africa, the volcanic 38-square mile island rises 6,765 feet out of the ocean surface in the form of Queen Mary's Peak, a massive shield volcano. First discovered in 1506, the island later became a trading station and wartime weather base.

*Rainier* was now making progress toward the tip of South Africa, and the Cape of Good Hope. The ship lucked out rounding the Cape of Good Hope, also known as Cabo das Tormentas, or Cape of Storms, for its ferocious storms and huge waves. *Rainier*'s passage went peacefully enough, with sightings of a whale, streams of dolphins, and several other ships, but none close enough to "speak," or identify.

Having "run her easting down," an old nautical term in which the suffix "-ing" was added to the direction in which a ship was sailing, in this case with strong winds from the west, *Rainier* was now headed directly into the Indian Ocean toward Australia.

Several other members of the crew, including the first mate, now fell ill. Suspicions focused on fumes from the kerosene tins, with some leaking from being tossed around during the voyage.[4]

By mid-October, Will Jackson had become the steward, as Silva's condition had worsened. Jackson himself complained of being very tired, partly from standing watch as well as performing the steward's duties. But he was becoming a key member of the ship: "going to the mate's room every other evening and have a chat," he wrote. He also was taking his meals with Captain Morrison, Humphrey, and Emma.

Despite rainy weather, *Rainier* continued to enjoy fresh wind, sailing smoothly, "running about 250 miles a day," Will noted on October 31. "We have made a splendid run from the Cape, about 6,300 miles in the last 30 days." They were now past the middle of the Indian Ocean, approximately 900 miles southwest of the southwestern tip of Australia.

The weather remained "squally, rain, hail," he noted in early November. But except for bragging that he had not chewed tobacco for three weeks and was "fatting up like a hog," the voyage went ahead smoothly. He noted they "expect to see Japan in about 2 months, Norfolk Island about 2 weeks." It is unclear if they had planned a stop at Norfolk Island, the notorious former British penal colony east of Australia. A need for more provisions and the illness on board provided logical reasons for the stop, whether planned or not.

On November 14, during a heavy southerly gale, *Rainier* overtook and passed a sleek, clipper-like ship, *Pactolus,* which had left New York as much as ten days before *Rainier* departed Philadelphia, also headed for Japan. The two captains knew each other well, and flags were dipped and handkerchiefs waved as *Rainier* sailed away from *Pactolus.* They were now 275 miles west of the southern tip of the island of Tasmania.

In one of his more expansive diary entries, Will described a keen sense of pride in *Rainier*'s performance. "She [*Pactolus*] was under small sail, but [in seeking to gain speed] commenced to make [add] sail as soon as we passed and is now under the same canvas as we are. [*Pactolus*] is considered a Clipper ship; we have gained 10 days on her so far. If we arrive first, we shall call it a good Beat."

Built in Thomaston, Maine, in 1865, *Pactolus* was actually not a clip-per ship but a graceful, full-rigged vessel, 191 feet long, at 1,205 tons, with an elliptical stern and carrying 5,500 yards of canvas in a single suit of sails. Carrying cargoes of lumber, kerosene, and phosphate rock through the Atlantic and into the Pacific, she was considered one of the fastest ships of the period.[5]

As *Rainier* passed Tasmania, south of southeastern Australia, the weather turned markedly warmer. At Lat. 43.23 So. Long 191.16 E, Jackson reported that the ship had traveled fourteen thousand miles from Philadelphia. His log reflected old problems, heightened anticipation.

On November 19, he wrote: "Row with cook this morning. Expect to get my head broke before I get through with him. Try to get along without too much fuss. On the home stretch now—making sail for Japan. All well."

On November 20: With *Rainier* headed north in the Tasman Sea, he wrote: "Everything as usual. Running to north and east. Making about 4 knots with a light breeze. Looking for Norfolk Island about first of next week. Out on deck sunning myself. Shall try to go ashore in the boat at Norfolk—to see the place. Am feeling first rate."

## CHAPTER SEVEN

# An Oasis of the Southern Pacific

WHEN THE SHIP *RAINIER* ARRIVED IN THE HARBOR OF NORFOLK ISLAND on November 28, 1883, the island was a well-functioning community with a flourishing farming system, a simple yet efficient road network, and a jetty built to allow ships to safely approach and dock. As they neared the island on the morning of the 28th from the southwest, Will Jackson wrote that the island "rises out of the ocean like a green oasis in the desert."[1]

Captain Morrison had decided that the stop, apparently unscheduled when they departed Philadelphia, was a sensible and timely detour. *Rainier* certainly needed more provisions and Morrison surely thought his crew deserved a landward break after three long and arduous months at sea. During recent weeks, several members of the crew had fallen ill, including his first mate Omar Humphrey, possibly from the kerosene fumes.

Norfolk Island, at 29.0408 degrees S, 167.9547 degrees E, is a small and isolated island in the southern Pacific Ocean that sits 868 miles east of Byron Bay, Australia, and 700 miles north/northwest of Auckland, New Zealand. The largest and northernmost of a three-island chain, Norfolk today has about 1,800 inhabitants living within 13.4 square miles of rugged, cliff-lined coast. The neighboring islands, Nepean and Philip, are uninhabited.[2]

Originally settled by East Polynesian seafarers in the thirteenth century, the island would be sighted and visited by the famous explorer Captain James Cook of the British Royal Navy on October 10, 1774, while commanding HMS *Resolution*. The fate of the early Polynesian settlers remains a mystery, but the British Royal Government made quick use of this remote island when they discovered the island uninhabited.

The British were attracted to the island not only for its proximity to Australia and New Zealand and the race to claim more territory than the French, but also for its abundance of spruce pine timber (Norfolk pine) for sail masts and for the New Zealand flax plant—to be used for sails and rope.

At the time, Britain was on the verge of losing a major source of timber from New England in the aftermath of the American War for Independence, so alternative sources were in demand. Furthermore, in 1786 Empress Catherine II of Russia restricted sales of hemp and flax seed to the United Kingdom on which the British Royal Navy was heavily dependent to maintain its naval superiority. Hemp and flax produced the cordage and sailcloth for all of the Royal Navy's ships.

The first European settlers to Norfolk Island, named by Captain Cook after Mary Howard, Duchess of Norfolk, consisted of nine male and six female convicts and seven free men sent to prepare for a larger settlement and commercial development. These first settlers were assigned several tasks, including the building of masts and sails and also to turn the island into a garden to help feed larger settlements in Sydney, then suffering from food shortages.

With convict labor, the new colony built the roads and infrastructure of the island and grew grains and vegetables. The colony would grow to over one thousand habitants by 1792.

The small community flourished—for a while. An American explorer, Donald Mackay, visited Norfolk during a long peregrination through the South Seas in the early nineteenth century. In an unpublished journal, he wrote on December 3, 1809: "While on shore, I walk'd out on the Island about 3 miles from the village and saw some fields of Indian corn equal to any we see in America—some fine pillars of wheat—potatoes and most of the Tropical fruit will thrive here. At present, the place is much on the decline, as the British government are about evacuating it—they have already withdrawn a number of the settlers."[3]

The Norfolk colony was abandoned by 1814 after failures of flax seed cultivation, the spruce pine timber, and various crops for a variety of reasons, among them salty winds, caterpillars, and rats.

The island remained uninhabited for a decade until the British Government decided to reestablish another penal colony, this time by banishing the worst of the convicts from New South Wales to Norfolk for the remainder of their lives. Many of these convicts traded a pending death sentence for their crimes in exchange for exile there. They called it "Hell in Paradise."

The British government abandoned the island again in 1855 only to send approximately two hundred residents of Pitcairn Island there a year later, including some descendants of the HMS *Bounty* mutineers. The latest settlers picked up where previous inhabitants left off, living in buildings of the penal colony and re-establishing the farming and whaling industries on the island.[4]

Will Jackson and the crew's experience on the island would be a pleasant one. In fact, Will would write that the time they spent upon Norfolk Island was the "pleasantest few hours of the voyage" to date. His gratitude no doubt reflected the hospitality and generosity of the islanders. He also described Norfolk as "a most beautiful spot of exquisite natural loveliness and with a climate unrivaled."

Shortly before dawn, while still dark, *Rainier* anchored off-shore, mainly to stay clear of roaring surf. To give notice of their arrival, the crew fired several shots in the air, prompting intense barking from dogs on the island. Soon, a man on horseback signaled them toward a safe place to land to avoid "a formidable line of surf."

At least two of *Rainier*'s longboats went ashore: one led by first mate Humphrey and another carrying another officer and Jackson. They were greeted warmly and immediately supplied with fresh fruit and flowers. Humphrey introduced the crew members who came ashore with him to the leader of the community, explained the ship's cargo and destination, and their desire to gain fresh provisions for the remaining weeks of their voyage. He gave the leader a number of copies of the *New York Herald*. And discovering that *Rainier* was the largest merchant ship to have ever landed at Norfolk, he invited a number of the islanders to go onboard to tour the vessel._

Meanwhile, Jackson and his unnamed shipmate rode in a horse-drawn cart to a ranch where they were cordially received by a Mr. Fletcher, who invited them to breakfast with his wife. While there, they also met a man from Philadelphia who had lived on the island for over twenty-three years and seemed "happy and contented." The man from Philadelphia also gave Will and his shipmate a "bouquet of flowers which were cultivated in great numbers and varieties" on the island.

After a breakfast of strawberries and cream prepared by Mrs. Fletcher, "the largest I'd ever seen," Will decided to have a look around. He came up with a remarkably comprehensive survey of the Norfolk community's social, political, and economic state of affairs for a visit of three hours.

"The island has good roads, splendid farms; the houses are not finished very well although they are great and clean. The people are kind and hospitable, each one owning the land he tills." According to Will, the islanders "live in perfect harmony with each other" and he offered praise for their prosperous condition. Will also wrote that they "seem proud of their island and their connections with the crew of the *Bounty*."

The Norfolk Island community supported a school, a church, and a single co-operative store in which all inhabitants owned one share. The 470 or so inhabitants included a minister, a doctor, a music teacher, an artist, and a chief magistrate who settled all disputes (so they were proud to say they had no use for a lawyer). Will noted that all residents had a supposedly equal standing in society but also observed that "women have not so high a standing as those of our country. Some are not allowed to eat at the same table as men."

First mate Humphrey reported that many of the women were native Kanakas, "copper-colored, of good build and fine looking."

Vegetables and fruit were plentiful, as was livestock, including cows, oxen, and sheep, plus geese, ducks, and poultry. The islanders had a three-masted trading schooner, which they used to trade for manufactured goods with the more industrialized islands of New Zealand. "Their occupation is tilling the soil, sheep and cattle raising, fishing and hunting the humpback whale. After the whaling season they have a grand Thanksgiving."

After Will and his shipmate finished their tour, which included the remains of the prison, they reboarded *Rainier* just before noon. Between them, Humphrey and Jackson had gathered a "boat load" of fresh livestock, including one steer, vegetables, fruit, and fowl. Jackson noted: "You can believe me that [one] did not have to be down in the state of Maine to have a Thanksgiving dinner."

That afternoon *Rainier* departed Norfolk Island and set sail for Hiogo with an eye on arriving in Japan in two to three weeks. Refreshed, resupplied, and bearing memories of a pleasant break, the crew of *Rainier* were all set for the final stretch run of a long and difficult voyage.

⌁

Not long after its departure, *Rainier* encountered the bane of a sea captain's sailing life: the doldrums—no wind. The ship made little headway sailing north/northwest into the long, north-south chain of the New Hebrides islands, according to Will Jackson's diary, encountering "calm, light winds" for nearly two weeks straight. "It is getting monotonous," he wrote at one point.

Illness still marked several men, including first mate Humphrey, who "had quite a siege." Will wrote that he looked forward to getting to Japan for two reasons—to get a doctor to examine the men and to receive some expected mail from home.

Healthy crew members "scraped the yard" and performed odd jobs on the ship to get it ready for Japanese harbor inspectors. When they weren't working, they were fishing for bonito—for sport. They had plenty of food now from their stop at Norfolk. "We look something like a farmyard afloat," Jackson wrote.

*Rainier* drifted for nearly three weeks through the Caledonia and New Hebrides islands. Finally, gentle breezes gave way to stiff winds, lifting everyone's spirits. Several small islands were passed as they entered the vast expanse of the Marshall Islands. Humphrey observed: "Now the ship was gliding along with a gentle breeze and the yards braced in. In two weeks, the *Rainier* would be safe at anchor."

On Christmas Eve, 1883, Will reported by his diary how much their stop on Norfolk had paid off. "Wish all a Merry Christmas. Tomorrow, I'm going to have a Norfolk Island turkey roasted, chicken stew, potatoes, turnips, onions, and Plum Pudding for Dessert. How is that for a bill of fare?"

Christmas day itself was rainy, squally, requiring the crew to work even though it was a holiday. As might be expected, Will longed for home; he said he spent his free time reading old letters. He also noted he wasn't feeling his best. But by December 31, he had cheered up. "Am feeling very fair, and back on deck. I shall be all right."

He then added: "Go on watch tonight as the steward goes to work this morning."

He closed his diary by wishing everyone at home "a happy new year to all and commence anew with the New Year. All well. R.W. Jackson (B.B.C.S.)."[5]

———

The ship's officers were now confident they were on the home stretch. Will wrote in his diary that he expected *Rainier* to reach Hiogo in ten to twelve days. First mate Humphrey reported that Captain Morrison came on deck in the late afternoon of January 2, after checking his charts just before supper, and told him: "The course is northwest, and we are now clear of all the islands at last, with nothing to trouble us until the shores of Japan heave in sight."

CHAPTER EIGHT

# "Breakers Ahead"

AT 3:00 P.M. ON JANUARY 2, 1884, THE ISLAND OF LAE OF THE MAR-shall Islands group had become visible on the port bow by the lookout on deck. With steady wind *Rainier* glided on and by 4:30 pm the ship recorded the island of Lae as eight miles distant by the cross bearing that had previously been logged.

Captain Morrison, confident of having cleared the Marshall Islands group, was optimistic in the near-term plan as he shouted the northwest-erly course direction to the officer on watch.

"Aye, aye sir," responded the officer, and moments later the supper bell rang.

The captain, before heading below for the evening meal, told the officer in charge of the deck to keep a good lookout for breakers until the ship was well clear of the island to the windward side and to keep a man at the masthead until dark. The second mate had the deck during this "dog watch" from 6:00 to 8:00 p.m., during which time the sun had set and *Rainier* continued to press on slowly through falling darkness.[1]

Supper was now complete and eight bells struck to signify the start of a new hour, 2000 (8:00 p.m.) and the commencement of a new watch. The first officer took charge of the deck and sent two men up to the top-gallant forecastle for lookouts, one of them being Will Jackson. By now, full darkness prevailed and in the far-off distance twinkling stars began to emerge in the high skies. The moon made a brief appearance in the eastern sky but set quickly and was now in retreat across other parts of the globe.

It was now 2030 hours (8:30 p.m.). The first officer, while making his rounds, found the captain on the mid deck peering through a telescope attempting to look through what had become an almost impenetrable darkness.

By 2100 (9:00 p.m.), or not long after, *Rainier* continued to charge forward under a heavy press of canvas through the South Pacific. Will Jackson was still in the forecastle with the lookout. Captain Morrison and the first officer stood on the weather quarter when the captain soon noticed something in the near distance

"That white ridge ahead looks like breakers!" yelled the captain.

At the same time the lookout's and Will's cries were heard.

"Breakers ahead! Breakers ahead!"

Every soul on the ship heard the shrieking calls and instantly appeared on deck.

"Hard a-starboard," Captain Morrison shouted to the helmsman. "Hard a-starboard!"

But it was too late! Despite the efforts of the first and third officers to let go all the port braces the ship was already upon the breakers and with a booming, terrifying thud ran full force onto a coral reef. Its bow was lifted into the air several feet; crew members fell hard on the deck, others barely caught themselves and remained upright while everything that was in a previously secured position was now scattered all over the ship. The ship and its crew were now in complete disarray.

As this catastrophic event was taking place and the ship rocked in all directions, the crew pulled themselves together and responded to Morrison's orders in orderly and disciplined fashion. Attempts were made to back the ship off the reef but it was evident that *Rainier* was doomed. Waves were hammering the ship and rolling up onto the deck as the sea crashed on the masts and poured down onto the crew.

The reef they had just slammed into was not on the nautical charts. It turned out to be part of the atoll of Ujae, a kite-shaped ring of islets, rocks, and reefs in the western part of the Ralik island chain of the Marshalls.[2]

Commands were given to carry all provisions and items of value from the aft to the front of the ship. This included the quarter boats hanging in the davits, which were in danger of getting smashed by waves or falling masts. The importance of these boats was paramount. Given the worsening condition of *Rainier* and the uncertain seas, the rescue boats were likely the only means of survival when daybreak eventually came. Everyone on the *Rainier* was in danger.

The Captain's daughter was one of those who remained calm, cool, and focused in the midst of this shocking event. She had been writing in her journal before bedtime when the ship struck the reef but was now calmly gathering key items, including those of her husband and father.

The heavy seas continued to pound *Rainier*, and the ship—a vessel of 1,877 tons, 233 feet long, 42 feet wide and 18 feet in depth—began to break apart. The timber on the hull was splitting and large cracks were appearing. The ship was now leaking badly and filling with water. Cargo began floating away, including the cases of kerosene, the piano, and other valuable provisions. The crew furled all the sails except the foresail and the lower topsail to keep her steady. It was very risky as the masts were whipping in the winds with every roll she made.

The only safe part of the ship was the bow, as the aft was now dropping lower into the sea and was almost fully submerged. The crew packed onto the front of the ship and brought as much cargo and provisions as possible as they attempted to make sense of what had just taken place and what the immediate future might hold. "The crashing of the timbers," a survivor later wrote, "gave evidence only too true that the *Rainier* was a doomed ship. The seas rolling on board presented a rather gloomy prospect of anyone being left to tell the tale."[3]

The remaining hours of uncertainty before daybreak were no less harrowing. The crew was stuck in the darkness upon a heavily damaged and sinking ship in the middle of the southwestern Pacific Ocean in unknown surroundings.

The crew certainly knew of stories that there were cannibals among the inhabitants of the South Seas. If they were to survive the remaining hours of the night, it was quite possible they'd eventually end up on a nearby island inhabited by "savages," islanders who, themselves, had had their own nightmarish encounters with white men who came on similar ships from the far side of the world. By the latter part of the nineteenth century, there was a long and established history of the slave trade in the South Pacific, which still continued at that time. Trading schooners would arrive at these remote islands, entice the natives to come on board then capture them and sail away.

Thus, with reason, natives of many islands would be distrustful of white people and maybe even anxious to capture—and even kill them if provided the opportunity. "All hands aboard a ship that was wrecked on an island thirty miles away in 1882 were said to have been murdered," one history reports.[4]

There's no doubt this was on the mind of the captain and crew of *Rainier* as they huddled on the ship anxiously awaiting the sun to begin its ascent and provide visibility into their surroundings and uncertain future.

They had rifles, they had ammunition, and they had each other but all else was, for the moment, completely out of their control. Their survival was—for the next few hours or days—up to fate and the gods to decide.

## CHAPTER NINE

# Among "Savages"—Fear and Reassurance

AS THE LIGHT OF DAWN BROKE ON THE HORIZON, THE CREW OF *RAINIER* could not have been very encouraged.

As far as the eye could see in any direction, north, south, east, or west, there was nothing but the blue Pacific, lines of breakers crashing on strands of coral reefs here and there. In the far-off distance, one or two small knolls of land could be seen.

Then, as the sun rose and daylight began to push away the gray clouds of the early morn, a few white sails appeared in the distance. As they came slowly nearer, they proved to be canoes of a South Sea island type, outriggers, crowded with "dusky natives," as first mate Omar Humphrey later wrote in *Wreck of the Rainier*.

Soon, the natives' canoes pulled up on the reef on which *Rainier* was slowly breaking apart. Unlike the night before, when the ocean depth was over the heads of the seamen, it was now low tide, and only a few inches of water deep on the reef.

With native skill, the canoes were quickly made fast to the reef, and several natives, all men wearing only a mat around their waist and coconut leaves and yellow flowers in large holes in their ears, approached the ship, shouting and gesticulating. It sent "a chill of terror to the unfortunate mariners who clung to the wreck which soon must go to pieces," Humphrey observed.

Captain Morrison and his officers quickly conferred, and not surprisingly, decided they had no choice but to try to communicate, negotiate, talk to the natives. They did have their stand of twelve Springfield rifles and a few other guns to defend themselves if necessary. The natives did not appear to have any weapons.

After Humphrey made some futile gestures to suggest that the natives swim to the ship, a long rope with pieces of wood from the wreck attached, a sort of gang-ladder, was thrown to them. Two natives finally grabbed the line and were hauled through the heavy surf, and aboard ship.

Humphrey recorded what followed in vivid terms:

"On reaching the deck they stood in mute wonderment and surprise, and on being handed a pipe and tobacco by one of the sailors, a broad smile played on their features, and with a grunt of acknowledgment they proceeded to fill their pipes after borrowing a sheath knife . . . and gave evidence they were no novices in the art of filling a pipe."

The captain and crew asked them many questions in different languages—since the crew included nearly a dozen men of different nationalities. The only words they seemed to understand were English words such as "captain," "schooner," and "whiskey"—which suggested they had been visited by foreign ships, either naval or trading vessels.

The two natives moved to hand back the pipes after a few minutes. But when they were signaled that they could keep them, both men "held them high in the air and shouted with a hideous screech to their kindred on the reef." Within seconds, many other men rushed into the water and swam through the heavy surf, then were "hoisted onboard and fitted out as were their comrades, also with (pipes), shirts and dungaree pants."

Having learned that the natives' island of Ujae (pronounced "oodge-eye") was as much as ten miles away, Morrison and his crew decided to set several of their small quarter boats into the water and take as much of the provisions of the ship, tools, and gear with them as they could manage. Will Jackson injured his right hand during the transfers.

Despite rough surf, first one, then several of *Rainier's* small boats were loaded and, after patiently waiting for the right waves on the hand signals of the natives, were safely brought away from the ship, off the reef, and into the calmer lagoon, away from the crashing surf.

By late afternoon, a small flotilla of *Rainier's* boats and the natives' canoes was tied together and ready to sail. A sailor was placed in each of the canoes, while the remainder of the crew went in the ship's boats. While the crew outnumbered the natives, Morrison and Humphrey parceled out the weapons.

As they prepared to leave for shore, Captain Morrison later observed in a report, "the decks of the ship burst open and all the cargo washed out over the reef to the sea. Then the masts all went and the splendid new ship *Rainier* became one mangled mass of ruins."[1]

After large mat sails were raised on the canoes, the rag-tag fleet then sailed with "great speed," Humphrey reported, and soon approached an island—approximately three-quarters of a mile long and one-quarter of a mile wide, one covered with coconut trees down to the water's edge. To the anxious survivors, it was the vision of "a perfect tropical paradise." The natives called it Ujae.

It was now dusk, and with a large group of islanders, men, women, and children milling around them, *Rainier*'s crew huddled together on the shore, not knowing what to expect—perhaps "some evil manifestations."

But soon the leader of the island, the king, took them to his hut and made clear to Captain Morrison, his daughter, and officers that they could have his modest square house for themselves and their most prized possessions. The king also gave orders to several of his subjects and they soon returned with large baskets of coconuts. Coconuts not only supplied a soft, pulpy, and edible substance after being broken open, but the milk took the place of fresh water, which did not exist on the island.[2]

As Morrison's crew settled down in a makeshift camp outside the king's house, using sails from their ship as tents, the inhabitants of the island gathered to view their visitors.

They were most intrigued to see a lone woman among all the men. They touched Emma Morrison's rosy cheeks and long red hair, and gazed intently at her fashionable clothes, purchased only months before in Bath and New York City. "Mothers presented their children [to Emma], and all the savages seemed to admire the pale-faced damsel."

Night came quickly. Several crew members and natives built a large bonfire, partly with coconut husks. Three mattresses hauled off the ship were given to the captain, his daughter, and Frank Silva, the steward, who remained very ill and had been in the water for nearly twenty-four hours. "Sleep soon came to the weary eyes, but the savages still sat about the fire, and some continued to do so until the morning."[3]

## CHAPTER TEN

# Building a Schooner
# and Life among the Natives

ALL TWENTY-EIGHT MEMBERS OF *RAINIER* SPENT A RESTLESS FIRST
night on this remote and mysterious island. While thankful everyone had
survived the wreck, they were understandably fearful and anxious.

A steady rotation of watchmen was put on guard in case of a surprise
attack from the natives, their twelve rifles at the ready. But no attack
came, and in the morning the natives brought the men gifts of coconuts
and pandanus, a tropical tree fruit. They still appeared friendly. Little
came for free, however. As before, during the first meeting on the reef, the
natives expected clothing or a small trinket in exchange for food.

After the exchanges, and a breakfast of coconuts and pandanus, Captain Morrison gathered his officers for a meeting to map out a plan for
their immediate needs and goals. He set out three urgent objectives: salvage everything they could get from the wreck, including food, tools, and
any material that could be used to build a boat; discuss the best options
for seeking immediate help; and begin to build better shelter for the crew.

With the ship fast breaking apart on the reef, the salvage operation
was the most urgent. After haggling with the king over use of his own
large canoe, through limited English and hand gestures, an agreement
was reached to give him an ax and two rifles at a later date. The second
mate, Harry Whalen Drohan, then took six men in the king's canoe and
two other boats out to the wreck. Morrison's order was to "load the boats
and canoe with as much provisions as possible, and to get some light sails

to make tents and sails for boats." The group returned that evening after a dangerous but successful mission—"throwing pieces into the bobbing boats which lay under the lee of the wrecked ship." They brought back several old sails, salt beef, pork, canned meat, and some bread. But they also brought bad news: the ship was "fast breaking up."

Early the next day the group made one more salvage mission but returned with nothing but a few cases of oil, some more sails, and news that the ship was just about gone. Drohan recounted the mission and condition of the ship. "The three masts had gone and everything had washed up on the reef. We managed to get some lines and some of the square sails, cutting them off the yards. We took what sails we could to make tents to shelter us on the island."[1]

Relentlessly battered by waves, *Rainier* had split open from stem to stern and had broken into scattered pieces that were rapidly washing away. A tall, proud three-masted sailing ship, barely six months old, was now a complete wreck.

Captain Morrison held another meeting to determine the best way to seek help. He had learned from talking to the king that few trading vessels stopped at the island. He decided that an effort must be made to send part of his crew into the vast expanse of the Pacific "to secure assistance."

Morrison called for volunteers, as Drohan later wrote. "Every man held up his hand. The captain selected myself and four men to start for the nearest inhabited island."

Their instructions from Captain Morrison were as follows: Locate a German trading station at Jaluit, which "lay dead to windward" at an unknown distance, but estimated at three hundred miles. If that could not be reached, they were to run the vessel to Oulan Island which lay three hundred miles to the southwest. If that stop proved to be unsuccessful, they were to proceed to Ascension Island, then to any port in China to the west, approximately three thousand miles away.

*Rainier*'s German carpenter promptly went to work to fit out the longboat for the voyage. The entire crew pitched in to help. Using a reduced part of the spanker gaff as a mast, they rigged the boat as a sloop. The vessel was stuffed with provisions to last about a month, including eight cans of water that had been recovered from *Rainier,* a half barrel of bread, twelve one-pound tins of meat, a box of matches, five pounds of tobacco, and four dozen coconuts. The navigating equipment consisted of a sextant with a clock for a chronometer and a compass. The stranded crew wrote letters to "mothers, wives and sweethearts" using any type of paper that could be gathered and put into a mailbag to be carried on the boat and, hopefully, eventually delivered.

Drohan recounted the scene just before they embarked on the mission:

*All hands came to the beach to see us off—except the captain's daughter, who had been making a flag for us. She then came running, saying "hold on, until I give you the stars and stripes to wave, and God Bless You." [Emma Humphrey] handed me a union she'd made from a red shirt, a white sheet and part of a blue dungaree jumper. All hands raised their hats and cheered. We pushed the boat off and we started down the lagoon at half past 10 o'clock in the morning and bade them all goodbye.*

In a move to ensure the safety of the crew on Ujae, one of the king's sons was induced to go on the voyage as the natives would surely wait for his safe return and thus not harm the stranded crew members. However, when the boat ran out down the lagoon on the morning of January 11, a day late due to rough seas, with the water still choppy, the king's son claimed seasickness, jumped off the boat and swam back to shore. So much for securing the safety of the men on the island. However, barring any unpredictable behavior by the natives, the remaining twenty-three members of *Rainier* appeared to be in good shape. It could be weeks, if not months, before they would know if the longboat mission would be a success.

In fact, Captain Morrison later described their immediate feeling: "After they were gone, we were like prisoners on the island."

In the next few days, strong winds and rough seas gave rise to constant worry about the fate of Drohan and the longboat, prompting Captain

Morrison to consider a more ambitious venture. He immediately began thinking of building a larger, more seaworthy vessel—perhaps a small schooner that could carry the rest of them to safety.

While he mulled over this idea, he set the crew to work building huts for more secure and weatherproof shelter. With some supplies from the wreck and planks from the island's trees, his men and several natives began building a series of small huts. They adopted the natives' design and construction.

First mate Humphrey described the work: "The houses are built of a framework of saplings put together without nails, being fastened by small rope made from coconut fibre, and thatched with leaves from the [various trees]." Several days were spent making the huts, and with the assistance of the natives, the process became much more efficient. A native could build a hut in about three hours—of course for the price of a shirt or pair of pants, by now the going cost of labor and supplies on the island. The natives, normally mostly naked, now were becoming more fully clothed; many members of the crew were beginning to resemble the natives with the daily diminishing of their limited wardrobes.[2]

Despite their skill in bartering, and a certain penchant for theft, the natives remained friendly, accommodating, and helpful. Initial concerns of a savage and brutal race of murderous cannibals had waned. In fact, the closest thing the crew had observed to unusual behavior was the natives' habit of sucking out the eyes and brains of raw fish after a successful fishing mission. Natives also ate the eggs of gulls when they were nearly ready to hatch, but both these culinary tendencies were undoubtedly delicacies on a tropical island offering little other than plants, fish, roots, coconuts, and breadfruit for food.

Partly due to their limited diet and seafaring lifestyle, the natives were a fit and attractive group. Humphrey described the appearance of the natives: "No finer race exists in the world as regards to physical structure. The men are tall and well formed. The women have magnificent proportions, pleasing faces and are neither flabby nor fat, and the contour of their bodies was harmonious and voluptuous." The women wore two mats below the waist, the men only one.

The natives were wonderful swimmers, top-notch sailors, expert fishermen—and the young ones could shimmy up to the top of a coconut tree with ease.

On any afternoon "a dozen or more [children] could be seen playing in the water and sailing their little canoes, and sometimes it seemed more like a civilized place than it did to be among savages, expecting every moment a spear to whiz through the air and pin you to the ground."

The natives were quick to learn and to adopt some of what the *Rainier*'s crew introduced to the islanders. Familiar with tobacco and red meat from previous encounters with trading vessels, the natives had a strong hankering for both and took advantage of any opportunity to indulge. The natives also copied the crew's method of making lamps by taking a coconut shell and filling it with oil and using a wick by the unraveling of cotton canvases. Before long, every man, woman, and child on the island had a lamp.

The natives numbered from 100 to 150 and lived all over the island in small huts with footpaths weaving through trees and thick brush to connect them.

Many natives spoke a few words of English, and understood several more. The children, who were bright, picked up English words quickly. The native language was difficult but the crew made efforts to learn important words and phrases. *Com-o* meant "thank you," *emun* meant "very good." *Anana* meant "no good," *con-e-tuk* meant "come here," and *igo nor-tar co-bar-ta* meant "I want a smoke."

Once their anxiety receded, the captain and crew of *Rainier* came to live alongside the natives with a reasonable degree of comfort and trust. The natives turned out to have a number of firearms and lots of ammunition, obtained from traders who came to the island. But they were not skilled in their use and seldom were seen with them.

The *Rainier*'s members admired the skill and craftmanship of the natives in virtually any kind of construction or endeavor—whether their small houses, varied canoes, or fishing exploits.

Some canoes were thirty feet long, three feet wide, and as much as six feet deep, kept upright in the water with a large framework lashed across the top of the vessel with split logs at each end for balance in the waves.

No nails were used; coconut leaves were applied between the four or five pieces of wood cut from breadfruit trees, with the leaves swelling in the water to make the vessels watertight. Their only tool was an adze, made from pearl found at great depths in the coral reefs. With one sail, they could fly like the wind.

———

Naturally, fishing was a major activity, occupation, and source of food for the island natives. The fish were abundant in the waters, even visible in the curl of waves as they broke along the reef. On fishing day, the islanders worked as a team, walking into the shoals with long strings of coconut leaves to force the fish into shallow depths where others would spear them. They would catch large quantities to last for quite some time.

On nights with no moon, night fishing was another activity that yielded large numbers of flying fish. Carrying torches made from dried coconut leaves, groups set out in canoes, fortified by long pipes filled with oakum to smoke. Will Jackson and his good friend, the third officer, Bamp Percy, were especially fond of this sport.

Omar Humphrey described the practice in *Wreck of the Rainier* after accompanying Jackson and Percy on one trip. After drifting along the lagoon, the native canoes would "launch through the breakers out into the ocean. The sail[s] were then hoisted, and away [they] sped like a race-horse before the wind." Attracted by the torches, the fish would leap into scoop nets. The fish would "fly for the nets, striking us on the head and body, until it seemed like a shower of bullets from some unseen foe. The natives [had] wonderful dexterity."

Humphrey declined to join Jackson and Percy again, however, after they encountered a large school of sharks one night. "Big sharks with long, flat noses, with mouths big enough to bite a man in two, would come and strike the canoes," though the first mate said it did not deter his two young crew members who went fishing with the natives whenever they went out.

After all fishing endeavors, the king would oversee a division of the catch, and carefully give the *Rainier*'s crew as much fish as he gave his people.

The main trouble for *Rainier*'s crew came from the natives' "thieving propensities." Two barrels of beef that had been saved from the wreck disappeared slowly—one piece at a time—from a line hung to keep the meat fresh by exposure to the air. Articles of clothing would be swiped through the natives' ability to cut a hole in the side of a hut and take an item at night. Jackson and Percy lost a whole bag of clothes in that fashion one night. The bag from which the clothes were stolen was made of heavy canvas and the natives were able to leave it in the same shape after they took the clothes, so the theft was not discovered for several days.

The cook was especially victimized. One night, despite arming himself with a large stick by his bedside, he was awakened by hearing and seeing his trunk move slowly from his bedside toward a door as if by magic. He leapt up, but fell over the trunk, allowing the thief to escape. A few nights later, he awoke, feeling cold, to discover his blanket disappearing slowly through a hole in the side of his house.

⌐—⌐

The native religion appeared to be solely focused on driving away evil spirits. Without any clear occasion or cause, the natives would assemble for a colorful ceremony consisting of drum circles, with the women beating on tom-toms, chanting, even some unusual rhythmic dancing by the king, all followed by a grand feast. A few of the events seemed to have been touched off by changes in the cycle of the moon, a visit from a tribe from another island, or a successful expedition or undertaking of some sort by the natives.

Perhaps one of the most mysterious aspects of the natives' culture was their belief in the spirit Libogen. The origin and precise identity of this spirit was not known, but it appeared to be a human being who had passed away, likely a woman or a female child. What was clear was that the natives worshipped Libogen, and the spirit would come at times to visit the king and his family—the only ones who seemed able to communicate with the spirit. The invisible yet "talking" spirit would prophesize and provide insight into the future, and, as the crew would later find out, with occasionally impressive accuracy.

One day on one of his walks around the island, Captain Morrison discovered an old log, about fifty-five feet long, that might be used as a good keel and garboard for a schooner. This old log, seemingly washed up from hundreds of miles away, suddenly became valuable to the king, who demanded payment in the form of the captain's large overcoat.

Morrison soon sent for the carpenter again, and asked him to gather his tools. They included a small augur, two planes, two saws (one half-broken), two axes, and two hatchets. A sort of sandstone was found, a hole cut through it and mounted on a wooden frame. That was turned by a windmill fashioned by the carpenter—the first piece of machinery in what would become Ujae's first shipyard.

On Monday, January 22, 1884, three weeks after the wreck, work commenced on the schooner.

Two of *Rainier*'s smaller boats made another search of the wreckage of the ship, and returned with some planking and spikes. Several large breadfruit trees were cut by the natives—after another exchange of shirts and pants. Virtually overnight, the shipyard "presented a lively appearance" and, once in place, work on the schooner accelerated at a rapid pace.

Building a ship from scratch on a remote island with limited tools and supplies proved extremely challenging. One setback came on a final search of the *Rainier*'s wreckage when one of the quarter boats capsized in rough waters. Several members of the crew would have died if they had not been quickly rescued by the natives in a large canoe. Two axes were lost, leaving only two hatchets. The remaining tools, hatchets and saws, were very dull, so sawing was slow work and one man could split only a few wooden planks a day.

After a week of hard work, with the king sitting, watching, in the broiling sun in the captain's overcoat, a forty-one-foot-long keel was laid along with a three-inch garboard. Stem and stern posts were bolted to the keel. Three midship frames were then placed in position, a ribbon fastened around, and frames fitted in and bolted.

In seventeen days, the schooner was framed and ready for planking. Oddly, with a lot of planks lying in the yard, a number of natives now went down the lagoon to the wreck and set fire to the remnants of the ship. No reason was ever given, but work continued.

In another seventeen days, the schooner was ready for caulking, using oakum that had been retrieved from the wreck. The carpenter had no caulking irons, so pieces of ironwood were sharpened and used to drive in the oakum. The final dimensions of the schooner were forty-one feet at the keel, nine feet beam, and seven feet depth of hold.

By Thursday, March 13, after fifty-two days of labor, the schooner was finished and ready to be launched. She was christened *Ujea [Ujae]* and her name was painted on each side of the vessel in large letters, using a dye the natives employed to color the strips of leaves that formed the mats they wore.

The carpenter and his crew had endured many obstacles, but "Yankee ingenuity overcame them all."

The crew put the schooner on rollers and all hands gently guided her down to the water at low tide to sit in shallow water. As the tide and water level rose, the rollers and supports floated away and for an instant the schooner floated upright. But she immediately began to careen and quickly started to fill with water through the main hatch and began to sink. The work of fifty-two days looked like a complete failure. As the tide ran out, the water began to empty from the vessel and the crew bailed her out. They then righted her and ballasted her with sheet metal that had been saved from the wreck. It appeared they had corrected the problems without a great deal of effort, no doubt due to their combined knowledge of shipbuilding and seamanship. Several natives, watching the work with keen interest, repeatedly said "*Emun! Emun!*"—very good, very good.

The next day, *Ujea* was taken on a trial trip that proved successful, and she was now ready to set out to seek help and rescue.

The schooner was filled with provisions, including a huge number of coconuts, and sailed down the lagoon ten miles to Boke Island, and anchored. Its departure, however, was delayed by the death of Frank Silva, the steward who had been seriously ill for a long time.

Will Jackson was assigned to dig a grave for Silva's body, which was sewed up in mats and placed in a rude bier covered with an American flag. The natives followed the proceedings intently. Their methods of caring for the sick differed greatly from the crew's, as did their burial procedures. They regularly invoked the spirit of Libogen but also placed a huge pile of rocks on a grave—presumably to prevent a person from returning, in human form or in spirit.

Members of the crew, trailed by many natives, carried Silva's body to the northeast end of the island, where first mate Humphrey read a Protestant burial service.

## CHAPTER ELEVEN

# Jaluit—and Back

THE MORNING OF MARCH 17, 1884, A MONDAY, DAWNED FAIR AND pleasant. A light breeze came up in the early hours, just what Captain Morrison wanted if they were to sail to Jaluit, the nearest island with a foreign—or "civilized"—populace. It was an estimated 300 miles away to the south and known to be a German trading station.

Morrison felt there was no time to lose. Due to an apparent stroke, he had lost all speaking ability. He had no use of his hands, his legs were becoming numb. In addition, several members of the crew, and now his own daughter, were ill and all of their limited medical supplies were depleted.

Will Jackson was appointed to join Morrison on the voyage, and, in effect, command the schooner. With Emma ill, Omar Humphrey could not leave, so he stayed behind with eight other members of the crew. The second mate, Drohan, had gone off with four crew members in the longboat in search of help—their whereabouts still unknown. So, ten sailors joined the captain and Jackson on *Ujea*, along with two natives, including Lija Bucho, the king's son, to act as interpreters at any stops at islands along the way.

The king agreed to escort Morrison, Jackson, and the rest to the schooner, now stationed ten miles down to the northeast end of the island near the only clear exit from the lagoon to the open ocean. The king's canoes were loaded with the remaining provisions and equipment, including charts, sextant, chronometer, and compass.

As Will Jackson recounted in his two chapters of *Wreck of the Rainier,* "We immediately hove up the anchor and sailed out of the lagoon, and commenced to beat up *Ujea* close to the lee reef, in smooth water. The schooner worked and sailed well and toward night we passed the island close by, giving three cheers to Mr. and Mrs. H. and the remaining crew who were standing on the coral beach waving their hats."

As the schooner sailed into the evening darkness, the weather turned foul. Heavy squalls forced the crew to reef the mainsail. The schooner pitched and tossed, making several seasick. Will divided all hands into watches and lookouts through the night.

By daylight, the wind moderated, and with only intermittent squalls, the schooner was able to carry all sails. They made seventy-two miles by dead reckoning in the first day.

With favorable winds, they sailed seventy-eight miles the next day, passing by the island of Lib.

Will had to deal with two challenging problems in addition to unpredictable weather: Captain Morrison's failing health and the nervousness of the two natives on board.

Morrison, confined to a small room in the stern of the vessel, was now unable to sit up, so even less of an advisor in reading the charts on board. "I judged from his appearance he was falling fast, and as we had no medicine, we could render him no assistance," Will observed later.

Meanwhile, Lija Bucho and the other native were constantly climbing to the mast-head and searching for land—and constantly seeing none, with seas running heavier and rougher, concluded all was lost.

As night fell again, the seas continued to churn and the odor of kerosene brought for trade grew stronger, even *Rainier*'s experienced sailors were alarmed. The natives were more frightened. They shouted "No see Ujae. Bum bye Emid!"—meaning they all would soon be dead.

Yet by Friday morning the winds had eased again and the sun had come out in full. With a chance to review their charts, Jackson and Morrison determined that they had made another forty-one miles. With clear sailing, they might reach Jaluit by night fall. And they did.

Near 4:00 p.m., Bucho, still in despair and aloft again, suddenly shouted "I see, I see." It was not until sunset that any of the regular crew could see land, but there it was. "It is a singular fact," Will wrote in *Wreck of the Rainier,* "most of the natives have wonderful eyesight, as many times they could see a canoe coming up (on the horizon) a long time before any of the crew could."

Smiles of satisfaction broke out on the faces of the crew. Morrison came on deck to help guide the schooner close enough to the several islands of the Bonam group, a large circle connected by a coral reef, so the vessel could be seen in the morning from the shore.

In the morning, Will sailed the schooner along the string of islands, looking for one of two known deep channels into the lagoon, and the main station at Jaluit. After sailing several miles, a canoe was seen passing between two small islands. Pushed by a fresh breeze, *Ujea* soon caught up with the canoe—and a sort of race ensued, ending with a meeting with an Englishman who was employed at the trading station. He instructed them on how to find a nearby dock, and soon *Ujea* dropped anchor and was tied up alongside.

Jaluit consisted of several large buildings, including the German trading station, two saloons, one of which contained rooms, and several houses, many no more than huts. Soon after their landing, Morrison and Jackson were met by a German who identified himself as the consul for the United States, a man by the name of Pfeffer.[1]

Pfeffer proved to be what Will called "a fat, pussy [pusillanimous] Dutchman," a nasty man who directed them to one of the saloons and told them to speak to "Negro Tom," the saloon-keeper, about a room. That was about the last thing Pfeffer did to help them. When Will went back to the schooner to remove some of their key instruments, he found that Pfeffer had ordered the hatches nailed down and effectively seized the vessel as collateral because *Rainier'*s officers and crew had very little in the way of funds.

A man of few words, Will wrote in his account of the visit how he regained possession of the ship's instruments: "Obstacles are easily overcome at times, and so I got all of our things and deposited them in the captain's [room]." He then went back to the schooner, sailed it out to an anchorage offshore, and placed Lija Bucho and the other native in charge to prevent any further intervention.

Negro Tom, a tall "outlaw" from the Samoan Islands, "supplied all our wants, and when night came we lay down to sleep, knowing that, although among civilized beings, our troubles were not yet ended."

—◆—

And they were not.

Will Jackson succeeded in rebuffing Pfeffer's effort to take over the schooner. "Yankee pluck overcame Dutch bluff," Will wrote. Lija Bucho, the king's son, a willful young man, remained loyal to Captain Morrison and Will and they gave him temporary command of *Ujea*, armed him and told him to shoot "any person who insisted on boarding the schooner after dark without permission."

Otherwise, Pfeffer ruled the roost on Jaluit. Despite pleas from Morrison to help his daughter and others, he blocked any effort by Morrison and Will to send aid or to rescue their shipmates on Ujae. In return for any credit, he forced Morrison to mortgage the remaining cases of kerosene, the schooner's sextant, chronometer, and even pieces of clothing at 5 percent interest a month.

Several trading vessels arrived in Jaluit in succeeding weeks, but Pfeffer convinced them to continue on their business rounds and not go to Ujae with provisions or for rescue. Will was able to write several letters and get them sent off on the trading vessels. Morrison also sent off a short letter to Omar Humphrey, detailing Pfeffer's ruthless policies. He reported [in the letter that eventually made its way to Humphrey weeks later] that he felt "very miserable, can't speak yet."

Days passed. With Captain Morrison incapacitated, Will was effectively in charge of the crew. He had trouble with several men, all of them older and more experienced than he was. They had become accustomed to spending a good deal of their time in Jaluit's two saloons, but with little to pay for their drinks.

Yet, perhaps because of his youth (now twenty-two) and lack of experience, Will remained in good spirits. In an April 6, 1884, letter to his father, Will reported that he had traveled to several islands, some thirty or more miles away. He went out at night with the natives in their canoes, armed with torches and nets, to catch flying fish. He even speculated that he might take a job in the island's store if they agreed to pay him fifty dollars a month. And he remained optimistic about reaching San Francisco soon. "You must not worry about me," he wrote his father. "Give my love to all hands. Tell them to think of their ship-wrecked brother, in good health and not very forlorn, on the South Sea Islands."

Jackson continued to seek a way to get back to Omar Humphrey, Emma, and the other members of the crew on Ujae.

A bark *Estelle* arrived a day or two before he wrote that letter to his father. And in it, he reported that *Estelle's* captain had agreed to take the ten men who came with Jackson and Morrison from Ujae to his next destination, Hong Kong. Jackson and Morrison would remain, hoping to convince another ship to return to Ujae.

The very next day, *Lotus*, a schooner belonging to King John, leader of the island of Alni Lap Lap and head king of the entire Ralik chain of the Marshall Islands, arrived in Jaluit's port. A twelve-ton yacht formerly owned by a resident of San Francisco, *Lotus* had come to Jaluit from Alni Lap Lap under the command of that king's son to pick up medicine for King John.

After the intercession of an English saloonkeeper named Sanders, King John's son agreed to go to Ujae with provisions and medicine after their return to Alni Lap Lap—provided King John agreed with the mission. Even Pfeffer offered medicine and goods for the voyage.

Will Jackson and Lija Bucho and his companion were to sail on *Lotus*, and after a few days' delay, the yacht passed down the lagoon side by side with the bark *Estelle*, on its way to China. Morrison, too ill, stayed in Jaluit.

The *Lotus* arrived at Alni Lap Lap a day later. Will's reception exceeded his expectations. King John was congenial, and spoke some English. He readily agreed to allow *Lotus* to go to Ujae in a few hours and placed Will in command of a crew of some thirty natives.

Will decided to take a walk around the island, stopping to join natives as they ate their evening meal. But as soon as he returned to the King's home, the king suddenly said "[Ship], no go."

Unable to figure out the king's sudden change of mind, Will spent a restless night in a hut he found empty. He decided he would steal away in the *Lotus* by himself whenever an occasion offered a chance to do so—and double-checked to make sure his revolver was in working order.

In the morning, he found King John still unwilling to allow him to leave. But he soon discovered that Lija Bucho was the cause of the delay. Bucho had told King John about Emma Morrison's trunk of fine clothes that had been recovered from the wreck, and had contrived a plot to take them as plunder.

Now resolved to steal away on the *Lotus*, Will spent another long night before rising with the dawn. Taking a canoe, he rowed out to the yacht, still lying offshore. There he found Bucho and about twenty natives "jabbering as fast and loud as they could."

"I made up my mind it was about myself . . . and my plans were soon laid. Opportunity soon offered and I told Lija Bucho he 'too much lie,' at which he got mad. So quickly drawing my revolver, I aimed it at him. The rest of the natives, on seeing the revolver, gave one yell, rushed on deck and jumping overboard, swam for the shore. Before I had time to think, Lija Bucho followed."

With no time to waste, Will quickly cut the rope to the anchor. A fresh breeze was blowing and he could be away before any of the natives' canoes could reach him. Just as he glanced seaward, he saw a trading schooner sailing into the lagoon, now very close. Will hesitated.

When he saw a white man at the helm, he decided to cast his fate with the captain of the schooner—*Frangiska*. He went on board the ship after it anchored and met Captain Ryan, who told him he had come to trade with King John. After Will described his plight, committing himself and Captain Morrison to pay the king for use of *Lotus*, Ryan agreed to intercede with King John.

<hr />

After listening to Captain Ryan, who spoke to King John in his native Kanaka language, the king told Will he was free to sail.[2]

"My heart was full of joy, and I hurried the king as much as it was possible, so that at 4:00 p.m. I was sailing rapidly away from Alni Lap Lap, with thirty-five natives on board for a crew, [including Lija Bucho, now chastened by the king] with a fresh breeze and squally looking weather."

By sunset, the wind had died to a calm, but the squalls continued. A strong rush of rain nearly capsized the yacht, and it was only saved when the main halyard was carried away and the sail run down. That scared the natives and they urged Will to turn back.

Knowing that would ruin his plans, he objected and prevailed.

By midnight, a light wind sprang up and they neared an island, Namu. The natives insisted on stopping there, to which Will consented. It became a brief visit, however, when Will told them he would not go ashore with them, so most stayed on the schooner, fearful he would sail away—as he indeed planned.

When the natives returned, Will took the wheel and steered "west, half west"—and by noon was in "latitude 80 degrees north, longitude 167 degrees 50 feet east."

After a stop at another island, Lib, Will was determined to make no more detours before reaching Ujae. Knowing enough of their language, he overheard them talking about a three-day visit to the next island to come up, Lae.

He therefore remained on deck all night and day until he knew *Lotus* had passed Lae. Once the natives realized that they had passed Lae, they pressed Will to turn back. But while making no promise, he was able to bring the schooner to anchor in place during the night to avoid severe squalls. At 3:00 a.m., with new wind, Will headed for Ujae and by daylight the island was plainly visible.

Discovering the island was Ujae and not Lae, the natives, however, "got wild and shoved me below and locked me down and headed the schooner for Lae—or *in the direction they supposed it to be.*"

"I yelled until I was hoarse through the cracks in the hatchway to go to Ujae, or a man-of-war would come and 'bum-bum' them all."

Whether his threats or the natives' lack of navigational skill was responsible, *Lotus* soon was approaching Ujae. Will could see a canoe bearing the king coming to meet them. The natives finally released Will from his brief imprisonment after Lija Bucho, formerly inclined to betrayal, urged the king to order the opening of the scuttle, and Will Jackson was able to free himself and talk to the king.

But rather than relief, Will suddenly was discouraged. The Ujaen king was dressed in the uniform of a commander in the US Navy.

"Without asking, I knew that a man-of-war had been to the island and rescued Mr. and Mrs. H. and the remainder of the crew, and what was to become of me I could not tell." While Will considered the possible answer to that question, the king took a note out of his pocket and handed it to him, saying "Man-of-war come. Emma go. Mate go."

Will tore open the letter and read the note:

*USS Essex, April 13—Rescued from Ujea [Ujae] Island Mr. and Mrs. H and eight of the crew of the Am. Ship Rainier, wrecked January 2, 1884. Essex sails for Jaluit to search for Capt. M. and thence sails for Yokohama, Japan.*
   *A. H. McCormick, Commander.*

Will Jackson had missed the *Essex* by just two or three days. And he could only curse his luck for having been going back to Ujae from Jaluit when the *Essex* was going from Ujae to Jaluit to pick up Captain Morrison—and him! The two vessels had probably passed each other at a distance.

The *Essex*, one of the largest warships in the US Navy at the time, had been in port in Canton, China, when it received orders to sail to the Marshall Islands to rescue Captain Morrison and his crew. The orders were based on messages from the US consul in Hong Kong after a British bark, *Catalina*, had picked up *Rainier's* second mate, Mr. Drohan, and his crew in the longboat in the middle of the Solomon Sea east of Papua New Guinea in late January. Given that *Catalina* arrived in Saigon on March 3, 1884, and Drohan and his crew went to Hong Kong shortly thereafter, it is likely that Andrew Jackson learned—through the Sewall company's agents in San Francisco—that Will had survived the wreck and was still on an island in the Marshalls.[3]

While Jackson pondered his misfortune, the king said to him, "Man-of-war go. No come again."

Will recovered quickly. He replied: "Captain man-of-war speak bum-bye [roughly meaning drop bombs] he come get me. Man-of-war go Jaluit, come back Ujae."

The king then sought to reassure him. "Never mind, King good to Will Jackson."

Will returned to the island from the reef with the king in his canoe, and they were met by a large crowd of the natives. "They seemed glad to see me, and so I shook hands with them all."

He then arranged to have the extensive cache of provisions brought off the yacht—which had been sailed down to the safe harbor off Boke Island. The provisions were stored in the hut Jackson and Morrison had stayed in on Ujae and though many items had been stolen before, the natives did not touch a thing. It probably helped that upon his reception by the natives, Jackson had told them the *Essex* would be back and could deliver "bum-bum" (bombs) on the king, the natives and the island.

No sooner had Will reconciled himself to his fate, terribly disappointed to have missed the *Essex* but glad to still be in one piece, when he received more bad news. The king and most of the natives on Ujae were getting ready to make an annual pilgrimage to King John and Alni Lap Lap. Early the following week, the *Lotus* and all the canoes on the island sailed away. Only twenty native men and women, too old to travel, and Will Jackson, were left behind.

Will elaborated on his lonely isolation in the second of his chapters in *Wreck of the Rainier:*

*The king, on leaving, made me king of the island, and [told] all the natives left to give me all the coconuts I required.*

*I was now left with no means of escape, as all the canoes had been taken. So I could only make myself as comfortable as possible and wait for some trading schooner to come. My time was spent walking around the island, watching for the sight of some friendly sail and lying in my hut during the heat of the day smoking and thinking.*

*Unfortunately, I could find nothing to read except an old alma-nac, . . . .and I read and reread it through until I could quote it from beginning to end.*

He related that he had brought two boxes of tobacco, and shared it with the natives. In return, the natives were very kind, bringing him all the coconuts and breadfruit he could eat.

Three more weeks passed.

## CHAPTER TWELVE

# Ujae—and Back to Jaluit

WHILE WILL JACKSON SPENT HIS DAYS READING AND REREADING AN old almanac, smoking tobacco, and walking around Ujae searching for a sail on the horizon, all of his shipmates were safely returning to the United States.

Jackson saw out the month of April and into early May on the remote atoll, alone among a small cohort of natives who spoke no English. Captain Morrison, first mate Humphrey, his wife Emma, second mate Drohan, and the remaining members of the original *Rainier* company were on their way from Yokohama, Japan, to San Francisco on the steamship *Rio de Janeiro*.

Morrison, still in grave health, had been picked up in Jaluit by the warship *Essex* two days after it rescued Humphrey, Emma, and eight sailors on Ujae—just before Will had returned with a ship full of provisions to aid in their survival.

"A more pitiful object would not be imagined," Humphrey later wrote about Morrison's condition when *Essex* pulled alongside a dock in Jaluit. "Sickness had reduced him to a mere skeleton, and being speechless, it was impossible to express his gratitude to his rescuers.

"Father and daughter were clasped into each other's arms, and as Mrs. H. led him to a chair in the commander's cabin, many an eye was wet with tears at the sight."[1]

Already on board the warship were second mate Drohan and three of the four sailors who had gone off in the longboat in the first effort to seek rescuers after the wreck of *Rainier*. They had been picked up in the middle of the southwestern Pacific in late January by the British bark *Catalina*, carrying coal from New South Wales, Australia, to Saigon. One sailor, Peter Dawson, had died from exposure and, as Drohan later recalled, all of them were "reduced to skeletons" and had given up hope when saved by the *Catalina*.

After a brief attempt to sail for Ujae against rough seas, *Catalina*'s captain decided the best course would be to continue to Saigon and seek help there. Once in Saigon, Drohan and his three colleagues were sent on to Hong Kong. In Hong Kong, the American consul contacted the US naval commander in the region and he then ordered the *Essex*, with Drohan and his crew on board, to rescue *Rainier*'s survivors in the Marshalls.[2]

So, after three days in the port of Jaluit, mainly to load coal, and with his surgeon ministering to Captain Morrison, Captain McCormick's *Essex* sailed for Yokohama, Japan, on April 19, 1884.

Morrison later reported that they were "entertained with most cordial and generous hospitality by all the officers and crew." Humphrey recalled how the days passed "rapidly and pleasantly," with very favorable weather and the officers regaling their guests "with quaint remarks and funny jokes," poems, and songs.

A Lieutenant Reese composed a five-stanza piece, "Ballad of the Wreck," for Emma Humphrey's diary.

> The wind murmured soft o'er the ocean,
> The *Rainier* sped fast o'er the sea,
> With queenly and confident motion
> To a treacherous, pitiless lee.

> [Final stanza]
> The *Essex* bore down in her beauty,
> The watchers were welcomed on board;
> The navy has done but a duty,
> Sweeter far than is wrought by the sword.[3]

The *Essex* arrived in Yokohama on May 5. Captain Morrison and Mr. and Mrs. Humphrey were given rooms in the Hotel Windsor; a "grand dinner" was given by the officers, with tables "loaded with Japanese delicacies." Morrison filed an official protest (the legal term for a post-incident report) of the fate of *Rainier* with the United States consul on May 15, and a visit was paid to Tokyo before they all sailed a day later for San Francisco.[4]

On June 4, 1884, "The *Rio de Janeiro* steamed safely through the Golden Gate into the large and beautiful bay of San Francisco and came to anchor in Mission Creek to await the quarantine officer."

Referring to *all* "the shipwrecked people," Humphrey wrote in *Wreck:* "Once again on native soil, after nine, long dreary months of hardships and privations!" —after leaving Philadelphia.

He had forgotten one person.

Back on Ujae, Will Jackson continued to scan the horizon.

And one day in early May, about the same time the *Essex* was arriving in Japan, when Will felt he had been stranded "about a lifetime," his fate took a more promising turn.

A native came running to his small hut, shouting "schooner, schooner." Soon its sails made clear it was *Frangiska* and its Captain Ryan—the man who had interceded with King John when he had blocked Will from sailing from Alni Lap Lap to Ujae more than a month before.

Ryan was back to pick up a cargo of copra. Copra is the dried fruit of the coconut palm from which an oil is obtained that was widely used to feed livestock. The copra trade, producing a ready cash crop, was the backbone of island economies in Micronesia for a century.[5]

Finding Will once again in a lamentable situation, Ryan invited him on the ship. Will sold some wreckage he'd recovered from the *Rainier* to Ryan, and a day later was on board *Frangiska* as it departed Ujae and called at several trading ports—Cogohu, Namu, and the familiar Alni Lap Lap. They arrived in Jaluit on May 14.

Consul Pfeffer was no more helpful than before. "I told him I was an American seaman in distress, and wished to be sent to an American port, which was his duty to do if American consul. He refused to have anything to do with me."

Repeated haggling did gain Will a hut to stay in, and he even shared meals with Pfeffer, who had an excellent native cook.

Pfeffer hired Jackson to paint his house at an attractive rate of $1.50 per day. The new owner of the homemade schooner *Ujea*, which Pfeffer had seized from Morrison as a security payment, also hired Will as a carpenter. Will put new beams in the vessel, caulked her, and made new sails. He was offered command of the schooner, to trade in the islands, but he declined. An Irishman on the island, Will observed with wry humor, had told him, "I might wake up some fine morning to find I had been killed!"

Trading schooners arrived constantly—but none were "bound for civilization." One ship came with barrels of kerosene and a chair—eerily marked "*Rainier*"—it had picked up three hundred miles away.

Will continued to correspond with his father and family in Bath. An August 9, 1884, edition of the *Bath Daily Times* reported this news under its "Society Gossip" column: "Will Jackson writes home that he is going into business at the Marshall Islands. Will was in the *Rainier*, it will be remembered. Send a Bath boy to the North Pole and in two weeks he would be settling there and running a barber shop."

A September 6, 1884, item in the same newspaper reported that "Will Jackson is making money running a trading station at Jaluit, one of the Marshall Islands."

Fate did look kindly on Will one day. The captain of a trading schooner, *Nieu*, headed to New Britain, another island group, urged Will to join him on his next rounds. "The schooner being new, I thought it would be a fine trip, but I had plenty of work and so decided not to go."

Lucky Will—again! A month later, word arrived on Jaluit that the schooner had been seized by savages on an island and all hands had been murdered. "I deemed it a narrow escape," Will wrote, "and made up my mind to reach a civilized country as soon as possible."[6]

A Swedish warship stopped at Jaluit one day, with a royal guest, the country's prince, Oscar. He was taking a pleasure trip around the world.

Will Jackson, a number of residents, and Prince Oscar spent several evenings playing billiards and drinking beer in Negro Tom's saloon.

Days before the Swedish ship left, a German schooner arrived, sailing from the Gilbert Islands and this time not headed for other islands to trade but bound for San Francisco. No doubt eager to be rid of Jackson, Pfeffer sent him to the captain of the vessel, *Tlalok* —and he was successful in booking passage.

The day before *Tlalok* was to depart, another schooner arrived and brought mail for one R. W. Jackson. One letter was from Captain Morrison, informing him of his safe arrival—and partial recovery—in San Francisco.

On July 31, 1884, his twenty-third birthday, Will Jackson finally left the Marshall Islands behind. In his case, the "hardships and deprivations" that Humphrey had lamented had lasted, counting his return voyage of fifty-one days, a total of fourteen months—three months longer than his shipmates. He worked as part of the crew, without pay, to cover his passage.

As *Tlalok* sailed eastward toward San Francisco, Will treated all hands on the vessel to beer he'd acquired from the consul. "Once again, I was at sea and homeward bound, and with a fresh breeze the island [of Jaluit] soon disappeared from sight."[7]

## CHAPTER THIRTEEN

# "Can't Kill Will!"

A WESTERN UNION TELEGRAM REACHED ANDREW JACKSON IN BATH on September 20, 1884. It was brief—but contained very good news.

From Richard Willis Jackson in San Francisco, it said: "Arrived yesterday will sail next week with Capt. Murphy will write from *W.F. Babcock*, to Liverpool."

It is clear that Mr. Jackson was already aware that his son was alive and well and on his way back to the United States from his long sojourn in the Marshall Islands.

A number of maritime sources, including Sewall representatives in San Francisco, appear to have sent messages to Bath that Will was safe. The last survivor of *Rainier* to return, Will would be back soon from his prolonged stay on the station of Jaluit and a difficult, extended second "visit" on Ujae.

The telegram reflected a certain truth about Will. He didn't let any grass grow under his feet.

No sooner had he returned from a grueling and dangerous ordeal on an isolated island in the middle of the world's largest body of water, he was prepared to ship out again within days. The schooner *Tlalok,* which brought him to San Francisco, arrived in port on Friday, September 19, 1884, as Will reported to his sister Clara Jackson Lemont in a letter written two days later on Sunday, the 21st. A day later, he had a new assignment, and less than two weeks later, he was en route to Liverpool as third officer on another Sewall ship, *W.F. Babcock*, built in Bath the year before *Rainier.*

But first, he had serious business to settle.

Once in port, he went straight to the offices of Williams, Dimond and Company, which represented the interests of *Rainier* owner Arthur Sewall in the West and Pacific. He talked at length with "Oscar and Will"—respectively, the eldest son of Arthur Sewall's brother Edward, and Arthur's youngest son, now engaged as executives of Williams, Dimond, a leading shipping and trading firm. He completed formal details that would have been required for wrapping up a formal marine protest. Captain Morrison had completed the main report in Yokohama, Japan, in May 1884.

But the real business at stake was to make a claim for his outstanding pay, expenses, and a large sum of money he had gained during his ordeal when a crew of wreckers arrived on Ujae and hauled off a substantial amount of salvage, including copper wire, rope; two hundred cases of kerosene, and a sixty-pound bell.

The two Sewall cousins, Oscar and Will, should have been able to make a decision in the matter. After all, they owned a majority of shares in *Rainier* between them. But the matter was referred back to Bath and Arthur Sewall, a wealthy man but one known for a tight fist in fiscal matters, a shipowner who seldom took out insurance on his own ships. (Sewall family papers indicate that Sewall had insured *Rainier* for $45,000).

According to records, Will submitted a request to Mr. Sewall for $100 for his expenses and his role in returning $450 to the Sewall interests for salvage from the wreck. A payment to Will took a long time. Another source says Jackson turned over $800 to Sewall.[1]

—————

The Sewall cousins were of little help to Will in his pursuit of what he called fair "recompense" for his ordeal and return of a significant amount of money. But they did assist him in regaining a foothold in the maritime world.

They introduced Will to Captain James F. Murphy, master of the Sewall ship *W.F. Babcock*. "He offered me Boatswain Billet in the *Babcock*," Will wrote to his sister Clara two days after his return to San Francisco. "He carries no third Mate so I am about the same as a third officer. I shall go on board Friday or Saturday, and will probably sail first of next week for Liverpool."

After an upbeat account of a busy weekend with dinners, skating rink parties, and reunions with a lot of "home people," including *Rainier*'s first mate, Omar Humphrey, and his wife, Emma, Will shared his happiness at coming back to the United States after a harrowing ordeal.

He recounted his return briefly in letters home—how he just missed the USS *Essex* rescue of the remaining crew members on Ujae by three days, requiring an additional three month stay until "I got taken off." He said it was a surprise to him to read in Bath papers that he'd been happily "coining money" and "running a station" in Jaluit. "I left Jaluit on the 31st of July, the happiest birthday I've have had for years. I am in splendid health." He did later report that he had lost as much as 40 pounds during his ordeal, down to 118 pounds.

"You don't know what a relief it was for me to escape from those Islands. I believe I should have died if I had had six months more of it. Hardly an hour passed but what I was on the beach looking for a sail. But it is all over, and I am all ready for another rackett [sic]."

---

*W.F. Babcock* had rolled off the ways at the Sewall shipyard in Bath on November 23, 1882, a 2,028-ton, 241-foot-long three-masted square-rigger—built and launched just eight months before *Rainier*.

Named for a San Francisco merchant who worked for Cornelius Vanderbilt's Nicaragua Line, the vessel was immediately sent to sea to earn back its investment. It was designed by one of the most highly regarded maritime architects of the age, William Pattee, a Bath native who grew up building miniature ships in his father's loft, and built by Elisha P. Mallet, the same shipwright who would build *Rainier*. The *W.F. Babcock* would prove to be one of the sturdiest "Downeasters" of the late nineteenth century, in service for more than twenty-five years across the globe. Maritime historians described the vessel as "one of the most prominent ships of her time."[2]

Her most regular itinerary took her from San Francisco to Liverpool and back, usually with grain or coal, a voyage she often managed in near record-setting times of 111 to 115 days.

The Downeasters—which one historian called "the highest development of the sailing ship"—were built almost exclusively in Maine. By 1875, historian William Avery Baker observed that "Maine shipyards" were delivering about 80 percent of the square-rigged vessels constructed in the United States compared with 51 percent in the 1850s.

Called "medium clippers," they combined large cargo capacity, great strength, and need for less crew with good speed—complete with the gleaming white canvas for which Yankee ships were famous. They were the perfect vessel for the booming California grain export business to Europe in the 1870s and 1880s.[3]

The author of a book on the San Francisco agent for the Sewalls, Williams and Dimond, noted: "The Downeaster contributed significantly to American maritime history, as it constituted the entire U.S. foreign-going merchant marine during the final four decades of the [19th] century."

James Murphy, an experienced master from a seagoing family, knew a promising vessel when he saw it. Thirty-three years old in 1882, with two decades at sea behind him, Murphy had been earning good profits for both the Sewall and Houghton firms for several years on transoceanic voyages with cargoes of wheat and coal.

Murphy was in charge of a rival company's ship when he boldly wrote to Arthur Sewall well before the *Babcock* was nearing completion. "Will here solicit and ask from you the captaincy of the new ship whose model you kindly showed me at your office. I may have taken too much liberty in asking you for such a ship, but my excuse is that I should like to command the largest and best ship out of the [Kennebec] river."[4]

A crusty seaman so well known for tall tales he earned a reputation as "the Great Liar," Murphy commanded the *Babcock* for eight years. The ship had just returned from Liverpool to San Francisco in August 1884 a few weeks before Will Jackson was invited to join the crew.[5]

Choice of the next "racket" for Will may have been heavily influenced by the prospect of engaging a position on a ship that would—even if by transfer to another—bring him to the East Coast. From Liverpool, it would be easy to reach New York—and get to Bath. His Bath connections also helped him gain a berth on a major ship at a time of listless business in San Francisco in the mid-1880s.

"Will have a lot to tell you when I get a chance to see you," he concluded his letter to Clara, who now lived in Boston with her husband, Frank, a photographer, and a new baby. "Will probably go to New York from [Liverpool] and take a run down home so you may see me home next spring."

Signing off with one of his typically idiosyncratic closings, he wrote:

*Your loving Brother, Will*
*Ex. – Capt. Schooner* Lotus
*Ex. – King of Ujea (Ujae)*
*And Present Boatswain of Ship* Babcock.

The *W.F. Babcock* departed San Francisco on the last day of September 1884 with a cargo of wheat and barley. R.W. Jackson was indeed the boatswain, at thirty dollars a month the fourth highest-paid officer after the first mate, steward, and cook, and a significant advancement over his initial twelve-dollar-a-month wage on *Rainier.*[6]

The ship's departure was delayed several days after a crew member complained of being cheated out of an advance to buy clothes—a fairly common experience.

The crew member, one Victor Gronquist, filed an assault charge against a "runner" for a boardinghouse, one Harry Mordaunt. Gronquist claimed Mordaunt had beaten him after an argument. The port commissioner, who had been ready to release the ship after inspecting its cargo, seems to have decided against Mordaunt and charged him. The September 30 report in the *Daily Alta California* is not quite clear, but Mordaunt appears to have been freed eventually.

Shipping companies and captains of the time often conspired with boardinghouses to fill out crews for their ships and long voyages. They hired tough guys like Mordaunt—called "crimps"—to do their dirty work. It was a distasteful employment that involved visiting saloons and brothels, heavy drinking, unclear contracts, and situations where many crew members suddenly found themselves at sea, "shanghaied" as the term became known, at low pay, with little clothing.[7]

With Bath's prominence in the maritime world, Bath "boys" had little to worry about in this respect. One of the few complaints Will had about this upcoming voyage was that he could not vote in the 1884 election, in which a Maine senator, James Blaine, was the Republican Party's candidate for president of the United States,

In 1884, Democrat Grover Cleveland narrowly defeated Blaine after a bitter campaign full of personal insults and mudslinging. Cleveland, governor of New York, edged Blaine, thanks largely to a razor-thin margin of one thousand votes in his home state. Will, who had just returned from the South Seas but would now be shipbound, told a sister he "would like to throw a vote for Blaine, but he will have to take the will for the deed."[8]

<hr />

Once underway, "light and fine, easterly airs" pushed *Babcock* down the coast of California, followed by a "mess of calms and drizzle rain," then "fresh and strong winds," according to the log kept by the first mate, C.H. Newman. But several weeks later, as the ship neared Cape Horn, the rough weather for which the region was famous came in as the ship passed directly south of the large archipelago of Tierra del Fuego (Land of Fire) at the tip of the South American continent.

*Babcock's* passage around Cape Horn would offer Will Jackson a lot more to tell his sister Clara and his family.

The only route from the Atlantic to the Pacific in those days, Cape Horn was an especially treacherous area. "Sailing around the Horn was difficult, often requiring weeks to sail from 50° South Atlantic to 50° South Pacific in the face of gale after gale from the west with the blocks and rigging sometimes so coated with ice that the ships could not be handled."[9]

"The Cape struck fear into mariners for 336 years, until the opening of the Panama Canal," commented another observer. "Rounding the

Horn . . . became a rite of passage that no sailor would forget. Cape Horn's reputation as the wildest place in the seven seas has its origin in the tremendous storms circling Antarctica from west to east through the Southern Ocean."[10] Waves there can reach fifty to sixty feet high.

In January 1883, Captain Morrison and Omar Humphrey, master and first mate of the ill-fated *Rainier*, had lost the Bath-built ship *Oracle* in a terrible storm off Cape Horn. One sailor had drowned during the harrowing ordeal, described by Humphrey as "a perfect hurricane."[11]

On November 17, 1884, according to the ship's log, *W.F. Babcock* encountered winds, "blowing hard, heavy puffs," at latitude 57.05, longitude 67.15, not far south of the tip of South America (Parque Nacional Cabo de Hornas). By midnight, the winds had increased to "almost a hurricane." The sails had to be secured. The lower fore topsail was torn out of its bolt rope. High seas crashed against the galley doors and windows; a quarter boat and a dinghy were smashed to pieces.

What happened next is best captured in the journal of Maria Higgins Murphy, the wife of Captain Murphy who often accompanied her husband on his early voyages along with a son, Wilder, at this time five years old.[12]

A couple of days after the storm, Mrs. Murphy wrote a long note in her diary about "the terrible gale or hurricane," adding that she still had not "gotten over" how frightened she was. After a pleasant, sunny afternoon that Sunday, the barometer had fallen sharply and winds increased in the evening. "It was blowing as hard as I ever saw it, and a most frightful sea [was] boarding the ship in such quantities."

Then she wrote: "During the gale, Will Jackson, our boatswain, and a sailor had hold of the fore brace, and a sea washed them right overboard. They clung to the rope, and surprised the others very much when they came over the side on board again. It was a miracle they were saved. When the water has such force as to crush the sides of a boat, human beings do not stand much of a chance."

On January 25, 1885, after one or two more rough storms but none as perilous as that near Cape Horn, *W.F. Babcock* docked in Liverpool after a passage of 117 days. Captain Murphy wrote to Arthur Sewall that unusual easterly winds in winter "spoilt my passage;" but that he had arrived safely, adding "no accident whatsoever." Will Jackson, who might have had a slightly different assessment, collected his $123 pay for four months and three days at sea. This time he had reached his destination.

On February 7, 1885, the *Bath Independent*, one of several newspapers in that thriving Maine city, highlighted this compact report right next to a large ad for a local ice hockey game between "the Granite Citys of Hallowell and the Alamedas of Bath—General Admission 25c."

## CAN'T KILL WILL!
### Another Escape for Jackson

*Ship W.F. Babcock, Capt. James F. Murphy, which recently arrived in Liverpool, experienced a very rough passage. On the voyage Mr. Will Jackson, a Bath boy, who was in the* Ranier *[sic], was washed overboard (reportedly near Cape Horn) and narrowly escaped drowning, but was providentially saved by his being washed on board the ship again by a wave.*

Richard Willis (Will) Jackson
FREDERIC B. HILL

William Donnell Crooker
RICHARD S. HILL

Andrew Jackson
RICHARD S. HILL

The Crooker/Jackson mansion, Bath, Maine
FREDERIC B. HILL

Ship *Glasgow*, C&WD Crooker (1837)
FREDERIC B. HILL

Ship *W.F. Babcock* (nearly the same dimensions as *Rainier*)
COURTESY OF MARINER'S MUSEUM AND PARK, NEWPORT NEWS, VIRGINIA

Captain Samuel Morrison (Master,
Ship *Rainier*)

| 17 | Pitter Larson | Sweden. | 25 | 5 | 6 | " | " | 18 00 |
| 18 | Wm. H. Smith | England. | 49 | 5 | 7 | do. | do. | 18 00 |
| 19 | John Clawson | Denmark | 26 | 5 | 9 | Li. | Li. | 18 00 |
| 20 | Paoli Edoardo | Italy. | 28 | 5 | 8 | do. | do. | 18 00 |
| 21 | Romeo Castelli | do | 25 | 5 | 5 | " | " | 18 00 |
| 22 | Raffael Zantini | do. | 23 | 5 | 6 | " | " | 18 00 |
| 23 | Jakop Tollefsen | Norway. | 22 | 0 | 8 | " | " | 18 00 |
| 24 | Andrew Jörgenson | do. | 21 | 5 | 5 | do. | do. | 18 00 |
| 25 | Johann Erickson | do. | 21 | 5 | 6. | " | " | 18 00 |
| 26 | Ole Olson | do. | 24 | 5 | 9. | " | " | 18 00 |
| 27 | Chas. Anderson | England | 27 | 5 | 7 | " | " | 18 00 |
| 28 | Ynp Dahlberg. | Finland. | 32 | 5 | 10 | " | " | 18 00 |
| 29 | Otta Haughey. | Norway. | 21 | 5 | 10 | " | " | 18 00 |
| 30 | Haans Wilhelm. | Finland. | 28 | 5 | 6 | " | " | 18 00 |
| 31 | R. W. Jackson | Bath. | 21 | 5 | 6 | do. | do. | 12 00 |
| 32 | Thomas Williams | England | 23 | 5 | 4 | " | " | 18 00 |
| 33 | A. Johans son | Findland | 24 | 5 | 7 | do. | do. | 18 00 |
| 34 | | | | | | | | |

Ship *Rainier* crew list

Krakatoa volcano eruption (1883)

Norfolk Island

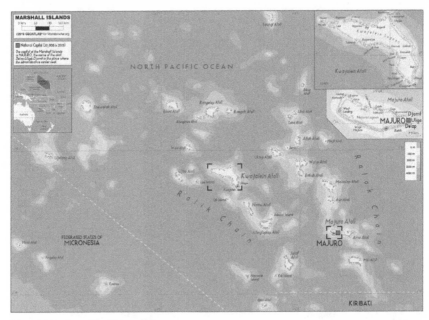

Map of western Pacific region

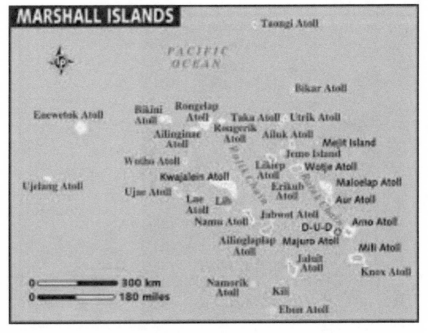

Marshall Islands map showing atolls of Ujae and Jaluit

Atoll of Ujae (with reefs on right and left in shadows)
PETER RUDIAK-GOULD, REPRINTED WITH PERMISSION

Six fishermen crossing reef on Ujae
PETER RUDIAK-GOULD, REPRINTED WITH PERMISSION

Tropical trees on lagoon, Ujae
PETER RUDIAK-GOULD, REPRINTED
WITH PERMISSION

Sailing with the wind, Ujae
PETER RUDIAK-GOULD, REPRINTED WITH PERMISSION

By the late 1880s, the harbor at Jaluit was crowded with ships. Freighters
and smaller vessels made frequent visits to offload supplies and pick up
copra. The ships carried the copra to major depots, like Samoa or Fiji, where
it was transshipped to Europe.

| previous | next |

Trading ships in Jaluit

FROM MICRONESIA: *WINDS OF CHANGE* BY FRANCIS X. HEZEL AND M. L. BERG.
REPRINTED WITH PERMISSION OF THE AUTHORS

Traders for an Australian firm are shown here weighing and buying copra in
the Marshalls. Competition was keen between trading firms to purchase
island copra throughout these years.

| previous | next |

Copra sacks (main trading crop)

FROM MICRONESIA: *WINDS OF CHANGE* BY FRANCIS X. HEZEL AND M. L. BERG.
REPRINTED WITH PERMISSION OF THE AUTHORS

Will Jackson's
telegram to his
father, Andrew
Jackson
FREDERIC B. HILL

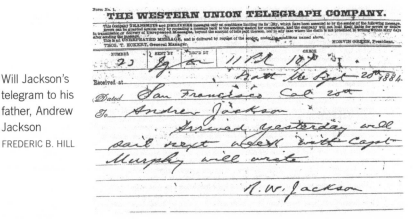

Pacific Mail Steamship Company dock, San Francisco, 1872
SAN FRANCISCO MARITIME HISTORIC PARK RESEARCH CENTER

Painting of ship *W.F. Babcock* by Antonio Jacobsen (1919)
COURTESY OF THE MARINERS' MUSEUM AND PARK, NEWPORT NEWS, VIRGINIA

A Ship at Sea: 4-masted bark *Vimeira*
MAINE MARITIME MUSEUM, BATH, MAINE

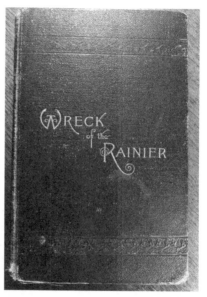

Photo of cover of book, *Wreck of the Rainier*
FREDERIC B. HILL

yesterday afternoon Feb- 7, 1885

## CAN'T KILL WILL!

### Another Escape for Jackson.

Ship W. F. Babcock, Capt. James F. Murphy, which recently arrived in Liverpool, experienced a very rough passage. On the voyage Mr. Will Jackson, a Bath boy, who was in the Ranier, was washed overboard and narrowly escaped drowning, but was providentially saved by his being washed on board the ship again by a wave.

Telegram: "Can't Kill Will."
PUBLIC DOMAIN

Ship *Gatherer* by Alexander Charles Stuart (1831–1898)
COURTESY OF VALLEJO GALLERY, NEWPORT BEACH, CALIFORNIA

Ship *City of Peking*
SAN FRANCISCO MARITIME NATIONAL HISTORICAL PARK (SAFR 21374)

Ship *Lakme*
SAN FRANCISCO MARITIME NATIONAL HISTORICAL PARK (K07.25.070P)

California and Drumm Streets, 1880
SAN FRANCISCO MARITIME NATIONAL HISTORICAL PARK (A14.35.784 PL)

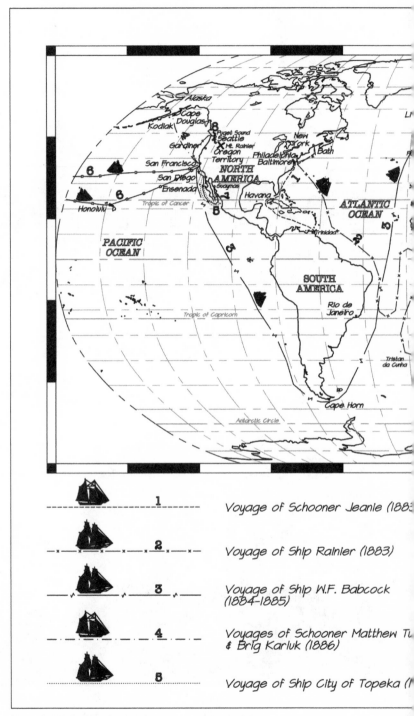

Map of Will Jackson's travels

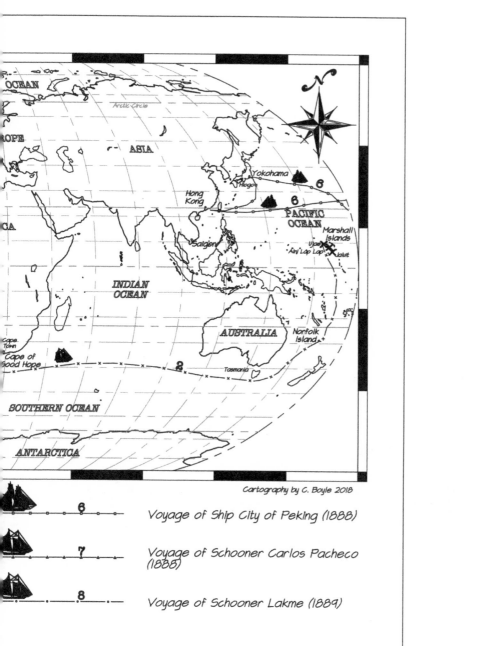

Cartography by C. Boyle 2018

Voyage of Ship City of Peking (1888)

Voyage of Schooner Carlos Pacheco (1888)

Voyage of Schooner Lakme (1889)

Richard Matthews Hallet
COLBY (COLLEGE) QUARTERLY, 1967

Marshallese shell necklace with beads, R.W. Jackson collection, 1884
FREDERIC B. HILL

## Chapter Fourteen

# Flat on My Back

With Will aboard, the *Babcock* returned to San Francisco on June 27, 1885, with a cargo of 3,060 tons of coal for J.D. Spreckels & Co., a large California steamship and trading company.

Unlike the outward-bound voyage, it was a largely uneventful trip after a violent storm hit the ship as it was leaving the Irish Channel. Mrs. Murphy, so frightened she "stowed herself down on the floor behind our bed," reported that her husband said it was "the worst sea he ever saw." Three young boys were discovered as stowaways; one was returned before the ship was far at sea, while the other two, ages sixteen and ten, described by Mrs. Murphy as "thin and forlorn, telling pitiful tales of poverty," were found too late to be returned and were basically adopted by the crew. At one stretch, *Babcock* made seven hundred miles in three days.

For Will Jackson, the voyage of 126 days went "very slow"—in part because he had had little word from home in England and, of course, none on shipboard for the four-month-plus return trip. And he still had no word of a settlement from Mr. Sewall.

Back in touch with his family once he returned to San Francisco, he informed his father that he was likely to be laid off as soon as the *Babcock* completed unloading its cargo. Captain Murphy was planning to put the ship in for repairs, requiring several months—meaning no salary.

Later correspondence revealed a more serious cause for leaving the *Babcock* and Captain Murphy, but Will did not mention it then—in part, he later said, out of concern that Bath newspapers would learn of it and hurt his prospects.

For now, Will was busy with three immediate challenges: one, to find another assignment, another ship, or to take a low-paying job on the waterfront; two, to settle the dispute over payments for salvage of wreckage from *Rainier* that he, and possibly, Captain Morrison and first mate Humphrey, had managed; and three, to see if he could rustle up some funds to help his father regain ownership of the Crooker mansion in Bath.

Clear ownership of the imposing twenty-room home overlooking the Kennebec River had been lost in the late 1850s when Will's grandfather, the once successful and wealthy shipbuilder William Donnell Crooker, went bankrupt and had stopped paying his property taxes. Crooker's father-in-law, James Robinson, himself a former ship captain, a large landowner and city leader, had begun paying them and held the mortgage for many years.

Thanks to Will's numerous Maine connections, things looked promising on gaining a new ship, if not immediately. A close friend, Walter Lowell, first mate on another new Bath-built vessel, *Gatherer*, had arrived in San Francisco, also from Liverpool. Lowell's father was the captain, and Will soon was offered the boatswain's billet, effectively third officer. The only downside was that he would be on half-wages until *Gatherer* found a new charter, and business at the time was "very dull here—lots of ships hard up." Like much of the rest of the country, San Francisco was emerging from a prolonged economic recession that lasted through the 1870s—called "the terrible seventies" in California—and into the '80s.

As a young single man, however, Will had no shortage of diversions while he looked for another assignment. Shortly after stepping on shore upon the *Babcock*'s return, he was invited to go hunting for two weeks in the hills north of the city, and he decided to go.

Settling the lingering dispute with the Sewall firm, Captain Morrison and Mr. Humphrey, remained more problematic. The precise details of the matter are obscured by a lack of records, but it is clear that the three principals had managed to save a considerable amount of material from the wreck of *Rainier*. In a detailed accounting Will sent from Liverpool, dated February 19, 1885, a formal statement, possibly compiled by a lawyer, gave this rundown of the salvage and $450 returned to "Mr. Sewall" from selling it.

| | | |
|---|---|---|
| *Bell* | *60 lbs @25 c* | *$15.00* |
| *Boats* | | *180.00* |
| *Copper* | *2733 lbs @5 c* | *136.65* |
| *Rope* | *1207 @4 c* | *48.28* |
| *Sails* | | *20.00* |
| *Oil* | *200 cases @79 and 1/2 c* | *159.00* |

In addition, Will claimed $20 in cash that he gave to "the chief" on Ujae, and $88.93 of "my expenses" during his prolonged stay in the islands.

His Liverpool representative quoted Jackson: "He adds 'I think I am entitled to some part of it, and whatever Mr. Sewall decides, he can pay it over to my brother Charles.'"

⎯⎯⎯~⎯⎯

Jackson did not claim past wages, but it is likely he had been paid those upon his return to San Francisco the previous year. At $12 per month, the lowest wage of any of *Rainier*'s crew, his grand total would have come to approximately $175 for fourteen months plus, unless his pay was upgraded as he was given ever more critical duties, including as *Rainier*'s steward.

Once back in San Francisco, Will pursued the matter—in a discreet manner typical of relations in that day and age between worker and owner. In a letter to Arthur Sewall in Bath, he wrote: "Please pay to my Brother Charles T. Jackson the sum of money which you have concluded to pay to me, on account of the wreckage of the *Rainier*. I think you mentioned $75 as a sufficient recompense. My idea was about ($100) one hundred dollars would be none too much whatever conclusion you come to. If you will pay it, to my Brother, you will oblige. Yours, R. W. Jackson."

Charles Jackson acknowledged receipt of seventy-five dollars from the Sewall company on November 6, 1885, according to company records.[1]

Will's letters home suggest that Morrison and Humphrey had already gained some funds from salvage of the wreckage themselves.

"It was a clear gain of $150. to them (Morrison and Humphrey)," he wrote once, "and I think they could very well afford to pay me something. I trusted to their generosity by handling it over there [in the islands]; I might have kept a part of it. In another week, it would have all disappeared. So I think if they pay me what is right by law, what is left is a clear gain to them."

The unresolved matter clearly rankled—all the more because Will was, as he related in several letters, just getting by.

Noting that he had been forced to buy clothes because he lost virtually everything in the Marshall Islands, he said: "The vessel [*Gatherer*] has not chartered yet, and there is no prospect of it doing so. I am still by her but . . . I am flat on my back out here and it is the best thing I can do to stick by her. Times are so dull."

Given his financial straits, he was clearly frustrated not to be able to help Andrew with the third challenge: "getting a settlement with Uncle James [Robinson]" on full ownership of the family home at 71 South Street.

"I would like to send you something," he wrote his father in one of several letters, "but have not got it. As for the mortgage, I don't see how I can do anything . . . though if you could get a settlement of the estate and there was anything in it for me, I would put it into the house. It is time things were settled one way or another."

After all, one could understand Will's desire to help regain control of the family's stately property. A major cause of his grandfather's financial collapse had been a swindle by a first cousin who took one of the Crooker ships around Cape Horn during the Gold Rush to capitalize on the thriving business on the wharves of San Francisco. His grandfather, William Donnell Crooker, and brother won a protracted lawsuit against the swindler, Henry D. McCobb, but the Maine Supreme Judicial Court's ruling that McCobb owed the Crookers $25,000 ($826,830 in 2020 funds) came years too late, after William Crooker had served his last term in jail, and was never enforced. On the very same waterfront where Will Jackson now waited to go to sea, McCobb, three decades earlier, had sold the Crookers' ship, *William Gray*, for a pittance, after having turned it into a storeship and then sunk it in the harbor.[2]

———

By nature an optimist, Will was confronting a challenging period in his young life. His wide circle of friends and "Bath folks," many of them extended families that invited him and others to dinner and parties, proved critical in keeping up his spirits. On the Fourth of July weekend of 1885, not long after his return from Liverpool, Will, Walter Lowell, and two other friends took part in a parade, visited a skating rink, walked through the new and sprawling Golden Gate Park and toured Cliff House, with its hundreds of seals thrashing about on the rocks—"attractions to the fashionable and wealthy."

They all then went to the Bush Street Theatre and enjoyed an oyster supper before "we cried quits with the Fourth of July 1885—not much like the 4th of July 1884 was [when he was stranded on a remote Pacific island], you can bet." In one letter, he noted "I have quite a home crowd around me."

Yet, he was clearly not happy. Six weeks later, in mid-September 1885, still standing by a charter for *Gatherer*, he shared much more of his frustrations with his father—and finally disclosed his problems with Captain Murphy.

"I am sick of this fighting to get a living here," he wrote. "I am going on 26 years old and am no better off than I was five years ago." He mused about returning east and working on coastal vessels again. (He must have meant "going on 25" since he'd recently turned 24.)

He then explained the run-in with Murphy. His explanation of the incident demonstrated remarkable courage and spunk on the part of an ambitious but still very young sailor vulnerable to demerits and mean whispers.

"You wrote that Mr. Sewall spoke as though I did an unwise thing in leaving the *Babcock*, but I guess he does not know the circumstances.

"I have not written the particulars because I do not want anything to get into the papers, but if Sewall says anything more, you can tell him that I say I would not sail with [Murphy] again in any position whatever.

"He tried a game on me here and it did not work well and I rather got the best of him, and it didn't sit well on his stomach—though he got into me for two days pay. When we got into port, I refused my money as the time was not correct. I went to him to have it corrected, and he allowed that it *was* correct; so we had a row and I had him called up to the [State Board of Labor] Commissioners and made him ante up."

Will added that Captain Murphy still owed him the two days' pay. "I don't think he will ever say anything about me, although if he does I guess I can tell as good a story. At any rate, I don't need any of his recommendations to get a vessel."

Will's aversion to Bath newspapers was longstanding—though he wrote occasional articles for them from distant ports. He just wanted to submit his own direct reports, not have news about him sent second- or third-hand. "I have learned that if you want to get along, it is better to keep a great deal that you know to yourself. And if you do not say anything, people can't say that you said this or that about so and so."

"When I get home, I can tell you more than I can on paper. If Murphy ever says anything, I will give him such an earache that he won't like it."

His ties to Captain Murphy and the *Babcock* broken, his trust in the Sewall clan strained, Will Jackson was nevertheless fortunate to be endowed with a tight circle of friends and a reputation as an able seaman of strong character and common sense. He would need his strength of character as San Francisco's "dull times" continued.

CHAPTER FIFTEEN

# The Bloodiest Ship Afloat

THE CITY OF SAN FRANCISCO IN 1885 WAS AN EXCITING PLACE TO BE despite a recent and prolonged economic downturn. Only four decades removed from a village called Yerba Buena, population three hundred, the city by the bay had emerged as the commercial, maritime, and financial capital of the West.

Blessed with one of the largest deep-water harbors in the expanding United States, San Francisco had been transformed from a "sleepy colonial outpost of New Spain" to America's gateway to the Pacific—and the world. From a remote post for otter pelt trading and the focus of occasional visits by Spanish, British, and Russian explorers, it was now a booming metropolis with a population of 234,000—the ninth largest city in the country.

Pedro Font, a Spanish missionary and member of an early party to find a settlement on the peninsula, observed in 1776 that San Francisco and its bay was "a prodigy in nature that is not easy to describe . . . and might well be called the harbor of harbors. If it could be well settled like Europe, there would not be anything more beautiful in the world."[1]

That "settling," in a city with one-fifth of the entire population of California, Oregon, and Washington in the mid-1880s, was now well underway. It was "a complex social mosaic" of New Englanders and Irish, German, Chinese, and Italian immigrants among others, revolving to a great extent around the bay.[2]

"The development of the waterfront defined early San Francisco economically as well as physically, generating an urban, commercial and mercantile core that allowed its developers and inhabitants to thrive in the face of competition, lack of available land, boom-and-bust economic cycles and a series of destructive fires. The founders of San Francisco were capitalists gambling on San Francisco's becoming a point of transshipment."[3]

There were several critical catalysts of San Francisco's and California's rapid growth, of course. It all started with the discovery of flakes of a shiny metal at Sutter's Mill near Sacramento on January 24, 1848, and the resulting Gold Rush—the "magic wand" that transformed the West.

News of the discovery of gold dramatically changed the state. In 1848, New York newspapers listed only six ads for vessels headed to San Francisco. A year later, 762 vessels departed the East Coast for the same destination. A literal "forest of masts"—abandoned ships—arose in the bay as captains and crews joined passengers on their way to the goldfields.

The transcontinental railroad was completed in 1869; oil wells began flowing in the 1870s. Agriculture blossomed in the state's fertile valleys.

California had to import its bread in 1850; by the 1880s, the state accounted for 43 percent of grain exports from the United States—the principal cargo of most of the oceangoing vessels that departed from San Francisco. Fishing and whaling also flourished, as did the lumber trade, dependent on coastal schooners due to the lack of roads inland both north to Oregon and Puget Sound and south to Baja California (Mexico).[4]

California had not become a state until 1850. While its seal highlights a grizzly bear (eating grapes) and the exclamation "Eureka" (Greek for "I have found it," namely gold), several large ships sail in the background—testimony to the pivotal role of the maritime world in the phenomenal growth of the state.

Given the Continental Divide, this sense of newness, even isolation from the East Coast and Washington, there was little thought yet of California as a full-fledged part of the United States of America. Early settlers, seamen, and immigrants revised an old Irish rhyme to fit the rollicking times:

*Oh, What was your name in the states?*
*Was it Thompson or Johnson or Bates;*
*Did you murder your wife and fly for your life,*
*Say, what was your name in the states?*[5]

⁓

Will Jackson could have found worse places to be twenty-four years old, on "half" wages and waiting for a shipping company to gain a charter to take a shipload of grain or lumber or kerosene halfway round the world.

It's not clear that he was aware of it, but he faced another hardship in the summer of 1885—as did Captain J.S. Lowell, and his son, Walter. And that was the recently tarnished reputation of the ship *Gatherer*.

A sleek, square-rigged Downeaster, a 1,509-ton, 208-foot-long three-masted ship, *Gatherer* was built in Bath, Maine, in 1874 by Albert Hathorn, a respected shipbuilder. It was, by all accounts, a beautiful vessel.

The 1874 *Nautical Gazette* raved: "This splendid specimen of marine architecture is one of the finest models and thoroughly built ships under the American flag." *Gatherer*, the article noted, was a stunning work: "copper-fastened throughout, (with) locust treenails going through plank, timber and ceiling, and wedged at both ends. The stern is elliptical and the head is ornamented by a gilt spread eagle. Black walnut, chestnut, oak and maple, highly polished, are the woods used in the cabin."[6]

Another observer remarked: "The superb quality of workmanship incorporated in Hathorn ships was exemplary of the masterful craftsmanship that brought maritime fame to Maine's Shipping City."

Under its first captain, James A. Thomson, the ship made history on October 1, 1874, joining three other new Downeasters as they departed Bath on the same day to head south to take cotton to Europe. Carrying hay as ballast, *Gatherer* reached New Orleans in thirteen days.

Though the cotton export market had declined sharply during the Civil War, it was returning slowly. Due to the low cost of sailing ships, smaller crews, and more cargo space, large trading companies continued to use sailing vessels for the international trade up until the end of the nineteenth century, even as Europeans shifted to iron- and steel-hulled vessels. *Gatherer* usually returned with coal to Hawaii, making eight trips around Cape Horn with a remarkable average of 129 days. These ships then came back to San Francisco, loaded grain, and took this increasingly essential export to Europe.

Downeasters, tall, three-masted ships, basically medium clipper ships with greater power and more space, were perfect for the grain trade. Taking their name from the region where they were built, Maine and northern New England, they had "a good turn of speed, [were] very strongly put together, and economical to work, yet requiring only half the men needed by an out-and-out flyer." *Gatherer* once covered 360 miles in one day, reaching speeds of 15 knots.

Will's problem, the Lowells' problem, was that *Gatherer* had not been under Captain Thomson's command for many years. By 1880 or 1881, the captain was C.N. "John" Sparks, with a first mate by the name of William "Charlie" Watts.

By 1882, Sparks had been relieved of his command and Watts and the second mate were in prison, prosecuted and convicted (or about to be convicted) of brutal treatment of their crew. Many captains were known for inhumane practices in the age of sail; many vessels were called "hellships"—with good reason. But under Sparks and Watts, the *Gatherer* became known as "the bloodiest ship afloat."[7]

According to various accounts and court testimony, during a long 1881 trip across the Atlantic and around Cape Horn from Antwerp, Belgium, to Wilmington, California, Sparks witnessed and encouraged his top officers, Watts and George Curtis, to repeatedly beat, hang from a mast upside down and withhold food from many of the twenty-four crew members, most foreign-born with little English. One seaman who protested conditions on the ship was shot dead; another, a young boy, was blinded by a belaying pin blow to the head and two more committed suicide by jumping into the sea. The third mate testified that "the deck of the vessel was never clear of blood upon it during the entire voyage."[8]

According to one grisly account: "A man named Swanson ran aft and jumped on the taffrail, stood balancing for a moment whilst he drew his sheath-knife across his throat and then fell headlong into the frothy white of the wake."[9]

Other sources offer even more detailed accounts of the inhumane treatment, such as William Chapman's *Sketches of Nineteenth Century Whitewash Civilization* (1895). Chapman commented: "A more fiendishly cruel man [than Sparks] never escaped the gallows."

Sparks, a master with a checkered past, was acquitted after a hung jury split over whether he actually did anything to the crew despite repeated testimony that he did nothing to stop the beatings by his officers. He was fired by the owners. Watts and Curtis, who carried out the "punishment"—they claimed for mutinous behavior—were both convicted of cruelty on the high seas and sentenced to six years in prison.

Watts's first trial in San Francisco ended on a technical reversal over the legality of his extradition—he had fled to Liverpool but was retrieved by detectives. As many as twelve seamen on *Gatherer* were held for nearly two years at government expense when the first trial was suspended. The *Daily Alta* opined: "About the only suspension the public would care to go in for would be the suspension of Watts at the end of a nicely soaped piece of 5/8ths Manila rope."[10]

The *Gatherer* case, which attracted standing room only crowds in the San Francisco courtroom and extensive newspaper coverage, was credited with encouraging formation of the Sailors Union of the Pacific in March 1885. The union quickly became one of the largest labor organizations in the western United States.[11]

—◦—

After Sparks, command of *Gatherer* was given to a Captain Simpson and then to J.S. Lowell. The ship eventually had peaceful voyages, but never overcame its violent history.

The "dull" times reflected the prolonged economic recession that had hit the country in the 1870s, hitting bottom with the Panic of 1873, and continued into the early 1880s. It affected the maritime and railroad business hard. A Bath newspaper reported in May 1884 that one million dollars' worth of Bath-built ships were sitting unemployed in San Francisco harbor. Other newspaper accounts of the period list dozens of "deep-sea vessels" as "disengaged" in the port for long stretches of time. *Gatherer* was one of them, unchartered from just after it arrived in mid-July 1885 from Liverpool with a cargo of coal. The ship had returned two weeks before the death of the country's eighteenth president, Ulysses S. Grant, July 23, 1885.

The *Gatherer* remained disengaged until January 8, 1886, when William Dresbach, a leading merchant known as "the King of the Wheat Pit"—later disgraced by scandal—signed a contract for *Gatherer* to take wheat to Europe, probably Cork, possibly Le Havre or Antwerp.

While waiting for owners of the *Gatherer* to put the ship to sea, Will took advantage of his free time to enjoy San Francisco and its many attractions—its skating rinks, professional baseball games, parks and zoo, dinners and parties with his friends and contacts from back home.

He had become a keen observer of San Francisco's rapid growth. He wrote home about construction of the new Palace Hotel, at fifteen million dollars and taking up a whole city square downtown. He marveled at the city's new cable cars—which he labeled "a great way ahead" of the horse and carriage. "You should see them go up a hill as steep as Walker's Hill at home. They're just as easy as going along a level. They have a cable all over the city underground that draws the cars."

With more time on his hands, he began to turn his attention to the young ladies of the Bay Area. In similar January 4, 1886, letters to his two sisters, he said "the New Year's racket" had "played me all out." Walter Lowell, also waiting on the *Gatherer*, and Will took two ladies to the theater, then while Lowell went to a cousin's for dinner: "I took the Ladies to a New Year's Eve ball. Got there about 11 and danced till fifteen minutes of four. I came home and slept all day, as we had a Holiday."

He even confessed that he might be thinking of settling down, telling Clara and Alice: "Think I shall have to get married if I can find any that will have me. Am looking around now for some rich widow, young and handsome."

He also began writing more often about being homesick. Asking for photos of his family, especially Clara's new son, regretting he had not been able to send birthday cards or Christmas gifts, he wrote once: "I am getting fairly crazy to see you all."

Early in the new year, 1886, Jackson moved to Oakland in the east bay where he would room with the first mate of the *Rainier*, Omar Humphrey. Humphrey, in one of the many coincidences of Will's life, was now captain of *Jeanie*, the Bath-built steam schooner on which Will first went to sea in 1883.

Will decided against shipping out on *Gatherer* with his friend Walter Lowell. He blamed small wages, and the prospect of a better position on an Alaska trading ship. Yet, in a letter to his brother Charles, he also alluded to another now common feature of the *Gatherer*. On the eve of departure, his friend Lowell had found a large part of the ship's crew drunk. "They got into a row, and [Walter] went to stop it and they all went after him. He got away with nine of them before the second mate got round, and they handcuffed them and locked them up. I wish I'd been there with him."

A June 3, 1887, report in the *Daily Alta California* underlined the long-lasting stain of the ship's reputation. Under a headline, "She Has a Bad Name," the account noted: "The American ship *Gatherer* is now suffering the effects of its infamous notoriety, as it is found impossible to ship a crew on her. Under former commanders, her decks have run with sailors' blood."

In terms of timing, missing the *Gatherer*—even after Captain Sparks and Charlie Watts—was another narrow escape for a lad—or "Bath boy"—named Will Jackson.

## Chapter Sixteen

# Salmon, Glaciers, and Grand Sights

Had Will Jackson been back in Bath in 1885, he'd have been happy to be home. But in Bath he would have had even fewer prospects of a good job—unless he was a master ship carpenter, and he was not.

If Will had been home in 1885, he like other residents would have been consumed by the botched hanging of Daniel Wilkinson, a British immigrant who had been convicted of the 1883 murder of a well-liked bank guard in Bath, Billy Lawrence. A poorly-tied noose led to a protracted strangulation of Wilkinson before thousands of spectators at the Maine State Prison on November 21, 1885, an ordeal that helped anti–death penalty activists to achieve abolition of capital punishment in Maine in 1887. Wilkinson remains the last person executed in Maine.

It was a tough time to find work. The long recession that had stretched out across the industrial world from a financial panic in 1873, aggravated in the United States by a speculative bubble in railroad construction and real estate, was hanging on. Business productivity picked up from 1879 to 1882, but had slowed sharply.

Shipbuilding, in Maine at least, remained an exception, briefly. It had recovered after the downturn that followed the late 1850s and the Civil War years, even though many of the region's skilled workers had left for higher pay elsewhere. New workers from Canada filled the void.

In fact, in 1882, partly because Maine shipbuilders had not yet turned to iron-hulled ships, "Bath was turning out a greater number of wooden vessels than any other place in the world."[1]

In that boom year, Bath yards launched more than seventy vessels. The transactions of Bath shipbuilders in 1882 with the famous London banking house of Barings Brothers ranked third in the United States, ahead of even Boston and Baltimore.

By May, 1885, however, the depression had hit even Bath. A sharp decline had been signaled by the bankruptcy of Bath's largest and most successful yard, Goss and Sawyer, in late 1883.

Only nineteen vessels were built in 1885, down from thirty-two in 1884 and fifty-four in 1883. A Bath resident wrote in a local paper of his sadness in seeing only one lone ship on the stocks of yards in the north end of the city, where he used to see twenty at a time. "She was sitting there apparently contented and patient, only waiting for her owners to complete their job and put her in the water."

One consolation for the city of Bath at this time was that it was no longer a one-industry town. Its economy had diversified markedly since the Civil War. There were two brass foundries, two sawmills, two clothing factories, a repair yard for the Knox and Lincoln Railroad, a coffee and spice mill, and a cigar factory.

Bath shipyards were to bounce back by the end of the decade, led by a reorganization of Goss and Sawyer into a larger, better-financed entity, the New England Shipbuilding Company, which partnered with the Sewall yard and others. While the end of the days of sail were looming, as iron- and steel-hulled ships were becoming more common, Maine shipyards continued to turn out the appealing Downeasters because of the lower cost (sail rather than burning coal) for the long fourteen-thousand-mile voyages from the West Coast to Europe with grain and other cargoes.

By early 1886, Will Jackson had prospects of not one but two positions; one on a new whaling vessel, *Karluk*, on which he was doing some maintenance work to keep an income, and another on a two-masted fur trading schooner, *Matthew Turner*, the namesake of the most prolific shipbuilder on the West Coast. The latter offer was for a first mate position under a Maine captain—but it depended on whether its regular mate returned from a current assignment. Both vessels would be headed for Alaska soon for several months.

Jackson was optimistic—as usual—that either billet would be fruitful and a next step in his climb to a command. "If I go in the *Turner* I shall not be back here until November or thereabouts. Will have quite a time up north. Would like to see you all, but must live in hopes. Hope I won't get into any more shipwrecks or anything of that kind."

Alaska was a new destination for Will Jackson. He had traveled up and down the East Coast of the United States, to the Caribbean, to Australia, Asia, and Europe. He would later serve on a number of vessels to Mexico and Guatemala.

He now made a number of trips north in 1886 and 1887 in *Karluk*, *Matthew Turner,* and a small schooner, *Maggie T. Morse.* The vessels were all under the control of the Alaska Commercial Company, headquartered in San Francisco.

One voyage went as far as Cape Douglass, a point southwest of Anchorage at the base of the Aleutian Islands, and Jackson enjoyed every minute of each trip. He or his father sent excerpts of his letters from various points in Alaska to Maine newspapers.

The *Bath Independent* ran a short article on August 14, 1886, reporting a twelve-day trip as second mate of the brig *Karluk.* "While north he saw snow for the first time in three years. He took the *Independent* up nearly to the North Pole and left two copies to educate the Esquimaux."[2]

Another article from Will about a later trip provided a more complete account. Under the headline "From Alaska," followed by a subhead "Telling about the Land of the Polar Bears," the *Independent* of October 30, 1886, reported "Wm. Jackson . . . was seeing the sights in the distant north, as a mate in the employ of the Alaska Commercial Co. He writes: 'We are working pretty hard now, running between Kodiak and Karluk with salmon. We were at Cooke Inlet recently after a hunting party. I have seen some grand sights in this part of the globe—one of the grandest which I ever beheld being a glacier near Cape Douglass.'" In a letter home at the same time, he added that he had run down the glacier, slipping and sliding over uneven terrain.

"It was like a large river of ice and extended up the side of a mountain until lost in the clouds, reflecting all the colors of the rainbow. On either side, the mountain, rugged and broken, extended to the sea. It made a wonderful, impressive spectacle. The country is tremendously wild, but its naturalness breaks pleasantly upon the eyes of an old traveler."

In a later letter, he said he would be headed back to Alaska in early 1887—and might be based there "on station" for two or three years. He said he would do his best to "come home to see you all."

—⁓—

With that anticipation, and no immediate prospect of an assignment, Will found his way home in November 1886, reuniting with his family for the first time since his departure on the ill-fated *Rainier* in the summer of 1883.

It is not clear how he got home—presumably overland, by train. But he had an added incentive to be there by the week of Thanksgiving. His younger sister Alice and Andrews Hallet were to be married on Tuesday, November 23, 1886, in a grand ceremony in the family home at 71 South Street.

The *Bath Daily Times* placed the story on its front page, an unusual feature, noting: "The spacious mansion of Andrew Jackson on South Street was the scene of a very pretty wedding last evening." Many of Bath's elite were listed among the "congratulatory company," along with a detailed list of their gifts, including Charles Davenport, leading businessman and political figure in whose name the Bath City Hall was later built, shipbuilder J.H. McLellan, William W. Pendexter, the J.D. Robinson family (which still held the mortgage on the mansion) and a prominent photographer, J.C. Higgins.

R.W. Jackson's name was at the top of the list of gifts with a dinner set. And, along with his brother Charles and older sister Clara (Lemont), he was one of a small group who rode in a carriage with the newlyweds to a reception and dinner in Brunswick before they departed on their honeymoon.

## CHAPTER SEVENTEEN

# "I Could Almost Imagine I Was Out There"

*In the year 1878, I took my degree of Doctor of Medicine of the University of London, and proceeded to Netley to go through the course prescribed for surgeons of the army. Having completed my studies there, I was duly attached to the Fifth Northumberland Fusiliers as assistant surgeon.*

THUS BEGAN *A STUDY IN SCARLET*, THE VERY FIRST NOVEL BY ARTHUR Conan Doyle about Sherlock Holmes and Dr. John Watson—who have become two of the most famous characters in popular fiction. Published in 1887 in *Beeton's Christmas Annual*, the novel, the first work of detective fiction to introduce the magnifying glass as an investigative tool, attracted little public interest at the time.[1]

Other notable works published in the year 1887 included *The Autobiography of Charles Darwin*, *The Diary of a Madman* by Guy de Maupassant, and novels by Thomas Hardy, Jules Verne, and Robert Louis Stevenson.

A small publishing firm in Portland, Maine, W.H. Stevens, struggled to get an appealing book on a shipwreck in the western Pacific on to the Christmas market for 1886, but failed. Its printers were overwhelmed with other business. The book, *Wreck of the Rainier*, covering the exciting story of a Maine ship, its Maine sailors, and their survival on a remote Pacific island, ended up being published in early 1887 instead, missing a golden opportunity to promote it in Bath and other cities and towns in Maine during the holidays.

Mr. Stevens, once described as "a bookman of the old school," apologized to Andrew Jackson for the delay. Writing to Mr. Jackson in March, 1887, Stevens said: "I'm sorry it was not ready when your son was at home. He seemed to be just the one to prove the truth by."

Will Jackson had finally made it home for his sister's wedding at the end of 1886 after three and one-half adventurous years at sea. But he had left Bath before the book was published, crossing the country by train and visiting friends along the way.

———

Back in San Francisco in early 1887, Will recalled "the nice times with pleasure" in a letter to his younger sister Alice and her new husband, Andrew Hallet. "You don't know how glad I am that I took the trip home this winter. I feel that the welcome I got from you all more than paid me for coming."

*Wreck of the Rainier*, published "by O.J.H." Omar J. Humphrey, the ship's first mate, was actually written by three people, in part due to the individual experiences of the officers and crew, who became separated during their extended stay on several of the Marshall Islands group. Humphrey wrote eight of the eleven chapters. Will Jackson wrote two on his separate adventures, and Harry Whalen Drohan, the second mate, wrote one on his rescue effort.

*Wreck of the Rainier* finally was published in late March 1887. The cloth, or hardback, version, was priced at one dollar, the paperback at fifty cents. According to a March 25, 1887, letter from Humphrey's brother, two thousand copies, a considerable number for those days, were printed.[2]

Andrew Jackson, who had traveled across Maine selling books from time to time in his varied career, placed an ad in Bath papers in April, saying "all orders promptly filled."

Short news items appeared in several Portland newspapers in late March. *The Portland Sunday Times* ran a brief article on its front page on March 20, 1887, under the headline "The Story of a Wreck." It read:

*Messrs. W. H. Stevens and Co. of this city will soon publish a new Maine book entitled* Wreck of the Rainier, *by O.J.H., an officer of the ill-fated ship. It is the story of a memorable shipwreck among the islands of the South Seas, with the natives of which the crew lived many dreary months.*

*A preface to the book is furnished by Robert Rexdale, author of "Drifting Songs and Sketches." The* Rainier *was a fine ship, built at Bath, and was lost on her first voyage to Japan.*

The *Portland Transcript* and the *Eastern Argus* published similar notices.

In a truly bizarre coincidence, a sailing schooner by the name of *W.H. Stevens* plied the South Seas in the very same period, frequently arriving in San Francisco to offload "South Sea Islands products." The *Daily Alta California* ran the following article on October 18, 1884, four weeks after Will himself arrived in San Francisco after his ordeal:

*The schooner* W.H. Stevens *arrived Thursday afternoon, 45 days from the Marshall Islands, with a cargo of copra (dried coconut kernels, from which coconut oil, used mainly for livestock feed, was obtained) and South Sea Islands products. She docked yesterday on Folsom Street to discharge.*

———

Will took his appearance in print in stride. He didn't refer to the book in several letters home until part way through a long letter to his father, July 6, 1887. He asked if his father had had any luck selling the book, adding he himself had not "due to cost." In a letter the same day to his older sister Clara, after regaling her with tales of Fourth of July partying and outlining plans for his next assignment on the steamer *City of Topeka*, off soon to Honolulu, he wrote:

*Glad you enjoyed the Book on the Wreck. You can imagine how proud I am to see my name in a book (a real live Book). I read it through the first night I got one and got real interested in it, everything seemed so familiar I could almost imagine that I was out there.*

———

Will's Fourth of July partying did produce "quite a racket." In addition to baseball games, the theater, dinners, and other get-togethers with his Maine friends, he and several mates nearly set off a major fire on the wharves in San Francisco.

During several trips to Chinatown, Jackson, Walter Lowell, Frank Webster, and one or two others loaded up on firecrackers. "I fired one from the steamer (*City of Topeka*) over on to a coal barge and it set the old thing on fire. The watchman put it out so it did not damage anything."

When *City of Topeka* did sail in August, with Lowell as first officer, Bamp Percy as second and Will as third officer, it headed not to Honolulu but south to Guatemala and ports on the coast of California and Mexico. The charter, carrying lumber, was for three months.

During this trip, Will encouraged his father to engage as an agent, or investor, to build a steamer for the Pacific coastal trade. He wrote that owners of *City of Topeka*, the International Company of Mexico, needed another vessel or two of the same tonnage, "seven or eight hundred tons," with "good freight and passenger accommodations."

"I thought they might be induced to build one down home [Bath]. As to iron or wood, I think cost would make a difference. They tell me the partners have money to back them, so that if they do take hold they mean business. Write to them as soon as possible, or get someone to, and find out what is what."

He added: "Perhaps you may be able to make a few dollars out of it." Will also had another angle in mind. If the International Company of Mexico were to build a steamer in Bath, "I should strike them to send me east to come out on her."

After a number of trips that fall south and back, between San Francisco and Guatemala, with stops in San Diego, Guaymas, and Ensenada, *City of Topeka* was headed north for its home port just before Christmas when fate intervened again in young Jackson's life, and, once more, turned it upside down.

Ironically, a Christmas disappointment led to a Christmas surprise: an overnight promotion to "Captain" Jackson, master at last.

## CHAPTER EIGHTEEN

# Prize Master

DURING A HIGH WIND, A SMALL, WELL-TRAVELED OLD WHALING BRIG, *Tropic Bird*, broke away from her anchorage in the dusty Mexican town of Ensenada de Todos Santos a few days before Christmas, 1887. The vessel, all 172 tons of her, drifted out into the bay.

It was the third time it had happened in the last week—events aggravated by the fact that the brig's new captain was reported drunk on shore, and its leaderless crew decided to abandon ship. Having retrieved the brig once, only to have her drift away again, the master (Rogers) of the San Francisco–bound steamer *City of Topeka*, in port en route north, appointed Will Jackson as prize master of the vessel. Rogers instructed him to take command until *City of Topeka* returned in a few weeks.

A British naval term, a prize master is an officer put in command of a captured vessel, usually in conflict, but also in cases of salvage or rescue.

Will Jackson had finally realized his life's ambition—if only in a most capricious, and temporary—manner.

Having reassembled its crew with the help of the US consul in Ensenada, "Captain" Jackson spent the day before Christmas and Christmas Day 1887 loading an overdue cargo of lumber from another ship and cruising around the inlet looking for two lost anchors.

Now sober and under restraining orders from the consul, the disgraced captain was returned to the ship, now as Will's "guest." In a letter home written Christmas Day, the new master said, "I have stowed him away in a spare bunk as I am occupying the Captain's room!"

A brief report in the January 6, 1888, edition of the *Daily Alta California*, simply noted that "R.W. Jackson, third mate of the steamer *Topeka*, was left to take charge of the vessel."

Despite his emergency promotion, Will was not especially happy.

"If I was looking for glory, I think I should sail her up to San Francisco [where *Tropic Bird* was heading]. But I don't want any old hooker like this. A dog her age would be no pup. I think she must be out of her teens [in age]."

Will wrote to his father that he hoped to break free of his duties shortly so he could catch up with *City of Topeka* in San Diego, its next stop, not lose his berth, and return to San Francisco.

He said he was "well and hearty," but "my X-mas dinner was what I call a failure, not even a piece of chicken or pudding."

Two days later in a letter to his brother Charles, Will reported that the search for the anchors was continuing to frustrate him. They had finally found the "port" anchor, but were still looking for the "kedge."

Before turning to personal news, he gave a blistering opinion of his new charge. "She is so contrary. I expect her to go to pieces in a strong wind she is so old. If she had hair on her head she would be pretty old and grey-looking."[1]

‒‒⁓‒

Otherwise, Will Jackson seemed content. He asked his brother if he'd hauled up his boats for the winter; he apologized for not getting back to San Francisco in time to send Charles his Christmas present, a box of Cuban cigars he had purchased for him. And he boasted that he too was growing a beard.

The most significant news was that a Bath friend, Walter Colburn, was in Ensenada, an officer aboard a new vessel, *Carlos Pacheco*. That turned out to be a very fortunate coincidence for Will.

Will signed off a letter to his brother with a P.S. from "Capt. Jackson of Brigg *Tropic Bird.*"

Weeks later, Will returned to San Francisco. By then the *City of Topeka* was in a shipyard for repairs, and he was out of work again.[2]

‒‒⁓‒

Not for long. And his new assignment must have made him think of *Tropic Bird* as a rowboat.

At 5,079 tons, 423 feet in length, the iron-hulled, screw-propeller steamship *City of Peking* was thirty times larger than the old whaling brig. *Peking*, like its sister ship, *City of Tokyo*, was the largest vessel ever built in the United States at that time.

It was built in 1874 by John Roach and Sons for the Pacific Mail Steamship Company, initially aided by one million dollars in subsidies from Congress. The subsidies were later rescinded as a result of a scandal but Roach survived the troubles and was able to build the ship without them. *City of Peking* encountered a rough trip on its maiden voyage around Cape Horn, but went on to a long and successful career as a passenger and cargo vessel and a troopship during the Spanish-American War.[3]

Will Jackson was now a happy man: Fourth officer on the second largest ship afloat (after a British vessel, *Great Eastern*). "Everybody thinks I have struck a good job" on the *Peking*, he wrote home. "It is the old story. Today I'm here and tomorrow somewhere else. Am in hopes to see Japan and China this trip; if I keep on at this rate I will do the whole world up before long.

"Was not looking for this job, but got it after my old style of taking the first thing I could get. I get along with the first mate so far; no work to do (that is physical work). Have to look after things but have plenty of men to do the work. Will be fat and lazy by the time I get back. It will be impossible to recognize me.

"Am in hopes to get ahead and lay up something for a rainy day. Hope I shall succeed in reaching Japan this time without any mishaps."

The *Bath Daily Times*, reported on April 7, 1888, that Will Jackson was "still bound for Japan" in an article headlined "Still Climbing." It reminded readers of the destination of the wrecked ship *Rainier* and noted that "Will, man fashion, has taken every job offered. Here's hoping our Bath sailor boy may some time be captain of the *Pekin[g]*."

While hardly a surprise, given his luck, Will just barely missed one of the few mishaps ever experienced by the *City of Peking* in its three decades of service. On March 4, 1888, a week before Jackson came aboard, the

*Peking* was in San Francisco under quarantine while its passengers and their belongings were being examined by port and health authorities.

It was common in those days for ships to offload their passengers and baggage to old, unseaworthy hulks where they would undergo the immigration exams, freeing the ship to move on. On that March 4th, the *Peking* was transferring passengers to an old ship, *Alice Garrett,* when the latter was swamped by high waves, and quickly sank. No lives were lost, but all the passengers' belongings went to the bottom of the bay.

*City of Peking* departed San Francisco on March 17, 1888.

Renowned for its speed, the *Peking* did not take much time in its voyage to Hong Kong, Yokohama, and Honolulu. Jackson was back in San Francisco in seventy days. Its return brought 1,400 passengers, mostly immigrants, to California.

Will said he liked the different cities very much, but expressed frustration that "I did not have as much time to look around as I should have liked."

Due to a lengthy quarantine on its return to San Francisco, he lost his position on the ship, "as I did not draw water enough at the office." Yet it turned out to be a good break.

Not only did he use the intervening days to study and pass the examination for first mate papers, but Will bumped into a ship captain who had been impressed by his brief command of the brig *Tropic Bird* in Ensenada six months earlier. The captain offered him a first mate's position on his ship, a coastal schooner, *Carlos Pacheco,* at seventy dollars per month, nearly double the forty-five-dollar salary he had received on *City of Peking.*

A friend of Will's, Walter Colburn, had been the first mate of *Carlos Pacheco* when they were all in Ensenada. But Colburn was now on another schooner owned by the same company, leading to the offer of his position, at least for a few months, to Will.

For the summer of 1888, therefore, Will had what he himself called a "soft snap" as first mate of the schooner, owned by the Mexican International Line, running between San Francisco, San Diego, and Mexican ports.

After one trip to San Diego, Colburn returned to the *Carlos Pacheco,* bumping Will down to second mate. But, within a month, the captain left on vacation, Colburn was promoted to captain, and Will was restored to the position of first mate.

In a clear sign of the widespread presence of seamen from Bath, Maine, Will wrote home: "So we are running now—Colburn (Bath) Captain, Jackson (Bath) first mate, Reed from Woolwich, Maine (a stone's throw across the Kennebec River from Bath), second mate, and Thwing of Woolwich as one of the quarter-masters. So you see we have quite a Down East crowd."

Will even urged his brother Charles to come out to the West Coast. "If he was out here, he could get a job, I have no doubt," he wrote to his father. "But he wants to be right on hand."

Newspaper accounts reported that Charles was having a high old time in Bath. He was working in a store owned by William H. Fogg, a store he would eventually own, and a store that was selling items brought home by Will from the Marshall Islands during his 1886 visit.

Charles had acquired "a large sailboat" in July 1886, and the *Bath Independent* reported that he was "passing his vacation yachting" down the Kennebec River and around nearby islands. He was captain of an amateur baseball team, taking sightseeing trips to Boston, and hosting dances with his future wife, Lizzie Merriman Stover, once leading "a grand march" of fifty-seven couples in one citywide celebration.

---

Despite continuing frustration with the pursuit of his overall career goals, Will Jackson remained optimistic. "Am feeling well, good food, no (hard) work, and $70. a month ought to make me in good spirits," he wrote to sister Alice. "Am having a very easy time as mate; only one more step to Captain's position. I have hopes of getting there sometime before I die. But I am satisfied for the time being."

## Chapter Nineteen

# "The Ways and Means of the World"

AMBITIOUS THOUGH HE WAS, WILL JACKSON WAS HONEST, EVEN-TEM-pered, and fair-minded. While dead-set on becoming master of a ship, he respected his fellow men, and women, and accepted a certain role for fate in his life.

Just after New Year's Day at the start of 1886, still seeking a position on a ship in San Francisco, he admitted his homesickness and frustration with his career to date in a long letter to his older sister Clara.

"Sometimes, I get discouraged, to think that I struggled to get along and when I think I am in a good position to get ahead and then have something turn up and upset all my calculations, to begin all over again. Here I have been 5 or 6 years trying my best to make something and am no better off than when I started—although I have got good experience in the ways and means of the world (more of the ways than the means).

"But I suppose there is no use giving in at all; the best we can do is to Hope On. Hope Ever. I am living in hopes and will probably die in Despair."

Yet, in his letter he turned to what he called "good prospect" of a billet—"going second mate in a fur trading vessel" in Alaskan waters in a few weeks.

Compelling evidence of his strength of character, his strong will, and determination to make his way on his own hook, is reflected in another letter a couple of years later. This one was written to his brother Charles from Astoria, Oregon, on September 30, 1888.

After updating "Bro" (as he called him) on recent travels and his misfortune to serve as a mate on a ship with an incompetent captain, he urged Charles to stop promoting his adventures back home.

"Another thing," Will began. "Don't give my whereabouts to the papers. I read a piece in the *Independent* about [my] 'Climbing Up,' as the headline read." Noting Jackson's steady acceptance of more responsible positions on ever larger ships, the article had promoted "our Bath sailor boy" as a future "captain of the *Pekin[g]*."

"I don't care about being made a damn fool of," Will wrote. "[The editor] may think it a smart little thing; it is not very pleasant for me to have a friend out here who gets the *Independent* and see the little pieces and know just how I am situated. They think I am writing them myself."

Noting that the newspaper had recently run three or four articles about his travels and exploits, some based on his letters home and turned over to the papers, Will urged Charles to tell the editor to stop using headlines and notes that made them "a high-flown piece about my expectations."

"I should prefer to have my name kept out of the paper. It does not pay to have a captain read in a paper that his mate, or second mate, or third, is expecting to step into his shoes. The editor may think that I like it, but I don't. What I write private, I want kept private." He was especially irritated at two items in the "Gossip" column of the *Bath Times* back in August and September 1884, published as he was actually en route to San Francisco from Ujae, that reported he "was going into business in the Marshall Islands" and "making money presiding over a trading station" there in Jaluit—both of which were an exaggeration of his real circumstances before he left the islands.

Will's aversion to publicity was reflected in another incident: the clash with James F. Murphy, captain of *W.F. Babcock*, the first ship he sailed on after returning to San Francisco following the shipwreck in the Marshall Islands. He preferred to submit his own account of any serious incident or quarrel.

Explaining why he left his billet on the *Babcock* after its return, due to a dispute with Murphy over his pay, Will told his father: "I have not written the particulars because I do not want anything to get into the papers."

"I have learned that if you want to get along, it's better to keep a great deal that you know to yourself."

Not only were his comments in these letters a reflection of a certain modesty, that he could make his way in his own good time, they also reflected how far and wide the men of Bath were spread in the world of ships and maritime commerce in that era. In the nineteenth century, when Maine and Bath were the among the most productive shipbuilding locales in the United States, its captains, mates, seamen, and agents could be found in ports and cities all around the world.

Historian William Fairburn observed: "Bath had so developed its shipbuilding industry and shipping interests that the name of Bath on the sterns of fine-looking, sensibly-modeled ships and barks was to be seen in all the harbors of the world."[1]

———

Although blessed with no more than a high school education, Richard Willis Jackson displayed many traits of a bright, well-rounded person. His behavior and personality reflected intellectual curiosity, willpower, and a wry sense of humor. He read widely, appreciated the wellsprings of a dynamic American culture, and wrote surprisingly clearly and succinctly. His diary's sketch of life on the remote Norfolk Island—after a mere three hours there—was worthy of a Ph.D. candidate's work.

Although on the high seas much of his adult life, a young man in his early twenties maintained an interest and engagement in the country's raucous political life, often commenting on a presidential election or the fate of one of Maine's leading politicians, such as Maine's senator and former Secretary of State James G. Blaine, one of the most powerful figures of the nineteenth century.

When in port, mainly in the bustling metropolis of San Francisco, he and his many Bath friends attended the city's theaters, skating rinks, baseball parks, and festivals. He went hunting and fishing in California's mountains and lakes. Furthermore, he was a loyal and loving family man—as reflected in his steady stream of letters home and frequent expression of concern for his relatives and friends.

Despite his lowly status, a seaman paid at the low monthly salaries of the time, Jackson stood up for himself in the face of unfair treatment—as demonstrated by his readiness to take on the Sewall clan and challenge Captain Murphy over a few dollars of pay he was due. For the most part, he made smart choices in very difficult circumstances—several times in the Marshall Islands and deciding against shipping out on the *Gatherer*—"the bloodiest ship afloat."

His quiet confidence and readiness to lead in challenging conditions were most evident during the long and sometimes harrowing nine months of his stay in the Marshall Islands after the wreck of his ship.

Will was the youngest member of the crew, one of the least experienced, and the lowest paid at the start of the voyage.

Yet he was assigned increasingly important duties, both during the *Rainier*'s trip from Philadelphia to its breakup on a Pacific coral reef and the ensuing challenges of survival.

First, he was chosen to assume the duties of the steward when Silva fell ill for the first of several spells. After the shipwreck, Will played a key role in the hodgepodge settlement on the atoll of Ujae. He was one of a few men who were assigned to retrieve provisions and items from the sinking wreck. It was Will who dug the grave for the steward after he died.

And then with Captain Morrison's failing health and the decision to build a small schooner to seek relief, it was Jackson who was chosen to command the jerry-rigged vessel *Ujea* on its perilous voyage among poorly charted waters. Quite a step up for a person who was at the bottom of the ladder in a company of twenty-eight five months earlier. At some point, Morrison had promoted Will to be his boatswain, or effectively, third officer.

During the next few months, due in part to bad luck, he endured far more rigorous challenges than any other member of *Rainier*'s crew.

Will was unlucky enough to be going in the other direction in the Marshall Islands as the *Essex*, missing each rendezvous, and thereby stranded for several months longer than any of the original crew. During one of the back-and-forth trips, he used his wits—and a shiny revolver—to face down rebellious natives.

His experience in the Marshall Islands clearly served valuable life lessons, preparing him for the "ways and means of the world"—the likelihood that fate was hard to dodge—and giving him confidence he could face whatever challenges lay ahead with courage and imagination.

While not particularly religious, he could be philosophic about his experiences. Closing the first letter he sent home after his return from the shipwreck, he wrote: "The old saying that Man proposes but God disposes has come true in my case."

By the time he was twenty-seven years old, Will had lived close to the nine lives of the proverbial cat. In addition to rescues of classmates in high school and being struck by lightning, he had missed the explosion of Krakatoa, admittedly by several weeks, survived shipwreck in the Marshall Islands, dodged enlistment on a ship in the Marshalls whose crew was later murdered, survived being washed overboard rounding Cape Horn on *W.F. Babcock*, narrowly missed serving on the "hellship" *Gatherer*, and outrun moving glaciers in Alaska.

Now, by late 1888, only five years after going to sea, after sailing from one end of the globe to another, he was nearing achievement of his life's ambition: master of a ship.[2]

For all his determination and willpower, for all the many hardships and tough luck, Will Jackson retained a keen wit, sense of humor, and generally optimistic spirit as he faced what by now he knew could be the unpredictable challenges that would come his way.

He frequently engaged his younger brother Charles in bets on who could grow a longer beard or broader moustache. He often mocked his own shortcomings, whether failing to stop chewing tobacco or making fun of his own appearance.

Once, after his return from the Marshall Islands, where his normal weight had dropped from 150 to 118 pounds and short on funds to buy new clothes, he had his picture taken and sent home. "You will not recognize me," he told one of his sisters: "I have grown as ugly as a hedge-hog."

He also referred to his wandering ways as making him "the Black Sheep" of the family, and told his sister Clara after one narrow escape that she "probably heard that the Bad Penny had returned to his native soil."

He shared his up-and-down exploits with his family with good, self-deprecating humor. In late September 1888, Will was serving as first mate on the schooner *Zampa* under a moody, down-on-his-luck captain. They clashed regularly during a trip from San Francisco to Astoria, Oregon, and back.

"We have a jam about every day," Will wrote in one letter. "One day he told me he thought I was an ass; I told him that two of a kind made a pair, according to Hoyle."

---

Despite his carefree attitude and independent streak, Will was beginning to think of settling down after five years on and off different vessels on the west coast. Not getting home more than once in that span, and missing his large family, it's not surprising that his thoughts began to turn to a more domestic life.

When he was in port, he was not always gallivanting around the Bay Area with his single seaman friends to the theater, skating rinks, and baseball parks. He frequently went to visit and enjoyed dinner with many married Maine friends such as Omar and Emma Humphrey, in Oakland, a ship captain Sewell Graves and his Bath-born wife, and the Wakeman family. The wife of Edgar Wakeman, a famous ship captain who wrote a well-regarded book on his adventures, *The Log of an Ancient Mariner*, was a cousin of Annie Jones Jackson, Will's father's second wife.[3]

A January 1886 letter to his youngest sister Alice, then newly engaged, found him ruminating about marriage. "Wouldn't you laugh to see Richard Willis getting married?" he wrote.

But for now, Will was focused on next steps. Having passed his exams and sailed as first mate on a couple of vessels, being named captain of a ship was now in his sights thanks in no small part to another adventuresome New Englander, a man from Connecticut who had been excited by the discovery of gold in California and moved to the West Coast and become a successful lumberman and shipowner.

## Chapter Twenty

# George Spencer Hinsdale

Nathan Scholfield, a civil engineer in Norwich, Connecticut, invented a variety of devices for cotton and woolen mills in New England. He earned patents for everything from sextants to harpoons to water wheel regulators. A successful entrepreneur and innovator, he had every reason to maintain the pleasant lifestyle of a country gentleman.

Yet Scholfield felt the same stirrings of so many young men in the middle decades of the nineteenth century as the country expanded westward. The Gold Rush may have been a final trigger. He went to California in 1850, and soon signed up for a major expedition to explore the Oregon Territory.

He was one of several engineers on the Klamath Exploring Expedition, underwritten by a San Francisco company, Winchester, Pope and Co. The group of fifty men set out to search the lower Umpqua River region of Oregon, an area passed by Sir Francis Drake and Spanish explorers centuries before yet still populated only by Native American tribes.

During their six-week stay, Scholfield and several companions encountered many wary native tribesmen, some hostile. Scholfield was credited with courageous leadership in facing down threats from several groups. In one instance, against his fellow explorers' warnings, he insisted on shaking hands, refused to show fear but occasionally displayed a revolver when the tribesmen came menacingly close, brandishing knives and stone hammers. The explorers withdrew to their canoes, but only after staking out land for future settlement.[1]

Scholfield returned to the lower Umpqua that fall and built a cabin on his land claim at the northerly bend of the Rogue River. In a letter he later wrote to the *Courier* newspaper in Norwich, he raved about the peace, beauty, and natural resources of the area.

*I can look out of my door or window upon one of the finest sheets of water on the shores of the Pacific, a Bay four miles in length by a mile in width, protected from the swells of the Ocean. Flocks of wild geese and ducks are constantly flying within shooting distance; also large flocks of pelicans frequently pass in review. Seals are gambling [sic] about with their heads above water, while large salmon are incessantly leaping their whole length out of the liquid element. . . . the solitude and silence of the night are not unfrequently broken in upon by the gruff growl of the bear, or some other wandering denizen of the magnificent wilderness.*

Whether George Spencer Hinsdale read Scholfield's report or not, similar accounts of exciting prospects in the West led two brothers, George and Sylvester Hinsdale, to leave their home in Connecticut in 1850 and travel across the country to seek fame and fortune.

The two Hinsdale brothers landed first in San Francisco, but soon found themselves in the Oregon territory. They set up a store in Scottsburg, twenty-six miles inland from the coast, to provide supplies to the gold mining regions in the mountains, at one point owning 1,500 mules, freight wagons, and later several steamships.

Even though Sylvester turned to seafaring for a number of years, the brothers' business interests expanded and prospered. They gained control of lumbering operations in the 1860s and began selling logs to a paper mill at nearby Gardiner. They eventually became managers, and partial owners, of the Gardiner Mill Company. Exploiting a coastal forest that ran four hundred miles north from San Francisco and thirty miles inland, the shipment of lumber became the most profitable business for coastal sailing ships with the end of the Gold Rush.

Not long after Sylvester's death in 1870, George Hinsdale expanded his business interests south to San Francisco, now the commercial, maritime, and financial center of the West and America's gateway to the world.

To the people of Gardiner, and Oregon in general, a later historian wrote, "San Francisco was the city from which we received our food, merchandise and supplies, and where many of our young people went for schooling or to find work."[2]

George Hinsdale soon moved to San Francisco, where he became general manager of the Pacific Pine Lumber Company. The firm owned several mills on Puget Sound in Washington, and set quotas that effectively controlled the lumber market. Its sprawling yards at Third Street in San Francisco off-loaded timber from coastal schooners, and handled sales to merchants, a lucrative business.

Hinsdale, by himself and with partners, also secured ownership of many of the schooners and steamers that ran up and down the coast, delivering everything from lumber to agricultural produce to needed tools. Smaller, two-masted, and maneuverable in small "dog-hole" ports, schooners had been the vessel of choice for many years due to their ability to sail close to an unmarked shore and into high winds. They also featured large space for cargo. "They were like the semi-truck trailers of our current day," observed James P. Delgado, a leading maritime historian. "In those days, there could be 400 of those schooners in the bay, waiting to offload or load."

It is not clear when Will Jackson first met George Hinsdale. It was probably in 1887 or early 1888 when Jackson was serving as first mate on *Carlos Pacheco*, a small steamer running along the California coast to Mexico.

Will first hinted at a possible acquaintance with Hinsdale just after he returned from the long voyage to China and Japan in the spring of 1888 as fourth officer on *City of Peking*, the massive five-thousand-ton iron steamship. In a July 15 letter to his brother Charles, Will mentioned that while he had lost his position on the *Peking* while it was back in port under quarantine, he had landed on his feet—in part due to his connections with Bath area seamen, and a new contact.

Not only had he passed his test for first mate papers, but a close friend from Bath, Walter Colburn, had just become captain of *Carlos Pacheco*, and named Will as his first mate.

Back in Mexico, Will complained about the foul conditions in the port where he was writing from, Ensenada de Todos Santos (Inlet of All Saints)—the same port where he had rescued the wayward *Tropic Bird* the year before. "Was out walking this afternoon. Came back covered with dirt. It is the dirtiest place I've ever struck." Then he mused that if he were to be replaced upon the ship's return to San Francisco, he was confident of getting a first mate's job on a new steam schooner. "I have had the promise of one whenever I want it."

That rare expression of confidence was a hint that he had met George Hinsdale, owner of several such vessels. Less than a month later, having lost his position on the *Pacheco*, Will was appointed first mate on a schooner, *Zampa*, a three-masted lumber carrier. Its owner? George Hinsdale. Its home port? Astoria, Oregon.

The new position proved to be a real challenge. His new captain, Will wrote home, "is the worst man I ever run across. He's always interfering; he's not had a mate with him for more than a month at a time. I thought it was rather funny the way the owners talked; they said if I did not like the schooner, I could leave her at Astoria. The captain and I have a jam about every day; it has got so now that we hardly speak as we pass by."

In the next letter, one to his father from San Francisco, dated November 23, 1888, Will was safely out of the *Zampa*, and now first mate of another, brand-new Hinsdale vessel, *Lakme*.

*Lakme*, a 529-ton, three-masted steam schooner, was built for Hinsdale in late 1888 in Port Madison, Washington, on Puget Sound. Steam schooners were larger and capable of maneuvering without sails, using steam winches to load and discharge cargo. *Lakme* was the first vessel of this type built in the Pacific Northwest. It was undergoing final refitting in San Francisco by Thanksgiving of that year, and Will was its "shipkeeper" until it would be ready for sea. He had a commitment from Hinsdale as the vessel's first mate.

Will described the ship, his "good job," and improving prospects in letters home. He also reported that he was spending some time with Omar and Emma Humphrey. Omar, now captain of the steam schooner *Jeanie,* Will's first ship, and now based in San Francisco, was delivering freight for the same company as the *Lakme.*

Will not only wished his family in Bath and elsewhere "a good time with plenty of Turkey, a merry Christmas and a happy new year," but also imparted telltale information about his relationship with Hinsdale as well as a second important, and romantic, interest in his life.

Writing late at night in shirtsleeves and a straw hat on a pleasant, warm day after a week of rain, he informed his father that he had been invited to Thanksgiving dinner at the home of a Captain Sewell F. Graves—whom he hoped would be given command of *Lakme* and its cargo of eight hundred thousand feet of lumber.

"He is a good friend of mine. His wife [Amelia Batchelder Graves] is a Bath woman (from nearby Phippsburg). Go to his house quite often, have lots of good times. He has three grown-up daughters." Thanksgiving dinner a few days later proved to be an important day in young Will's life.

After briefly reporting on various shipboard assignments of Bath friends, Will also passed on more news of his growing relationship with Hinsdale. "The owner is down to the ship every day, brings me the morning papers to read, and a magazine once in a while. I like him very much and I think I suit him."

———

It is very likely that Hinsdale, now often referred to as Captain Hinsdale, saw a lot of himself in Will Jackson.

Certainly Will's adventurous, can-do spirit appealed to the older man. The fact that Will had persevered through the shipwreck in the Marshall Islands, served on several tough ships, gained his first mate's papers, and faced down the churlish master of *Zampa* stood him in good stead. But another factor had to be at play.

Like Will Jackson, George Hinsdale's family had been beset by financial difficulties. His grandfather, like Jackson's, had been a successful entrepreneur for much of his life, a sea captain who then encountered bankruptcy and potential imprisonment.

Hinsdale's father, though having inherited some wealth despite the battle with debt, lost that in the banking business and investments in Hartford, Connecticut. Hinsdale's upbringing was haunted by early deaths: His father died when he was ten, and several sisters and brothers died in their thirties. Hinsdale himself went to sea at age fourteen, a few years after his father's death in 1832.

His brother Sylvester, his partner in several enterprises in Oregon, had died at forty-six during a trip back east. Lastly, George Hinsdale married Catherine Alice Putnam in Scottsburg, Oregon, in August 1854. She died the next year—and he never remarried.

Oregon histories mention that Hinsdale survived "a lifetime of turmoil," including a series of forest fires that damaged his business. Yet he remained actively engaged in his community, state, and region. A Republican, he served in the Oregon Senate in the 1860s.

A Hinsdale family genealogy, which takes the family back to France and the name de Hinnisdal, concludes: "He was very methodical in his habits. Circumstances made his life a lonely one."[3]

## CHAPTER TWENTY-ONE

# "A Good Sensible Girl"

THANKSGIVING 1888 AT THE HOME OF CAPTAIN GRAVES APPEARS TO have been a grand affair.

Barely a week after his last letter, after a ritual exchange of concern for everyone's health and details on the inefficiency of the mail, Will disclosed that he was now engaged—to one of Captain Graves's three daughters.

Backing into his news again, he began: "You say Charles is still a bachelor; well so am I, but I will tell you that it won't be for long, as I confess to you that I am in love with a very nice young lady and am engaged to her. I hope to be married sooner than later."

He said he would send a photo of the group from Thanksgiving dinner, and described how his father could identify Mattie Octavia Graves, nineteen years old.

"Take a good look at the one sitting in back of Bamp Percy's chair and you will see a very nice likeness of the future. I know this will surprise you all, but no more so than it did the young lady's folks. Her name is Mattie O. Graves; she is a relative of the Morrisons. Her mother was Amelia Batchelder, from Phippsburg, so you see if I don't get home to get a wife I will get a little Bath blood."

"She is a daisy—and would like to have you as a father-in-law. I hope you will survive the news long enough to send us your blessing." Mattie is, he added, "a good sensible girl."

Otherwise, Will's life was relatively quiet for once. He was still in port, as Mr. Hinsdale's *Lakme* was waiting for a propeller to be installed.

He said he was in good health, enjoying his stewardship of the vessel, where he had a night watchman so he did not have to stay on board at night. But, he added, he was eager to get to sea—delayed now probably until New Year's Day.

Having passed his first mate's exams, he was now earning seventy-five to eighty dollars per month, and confident he could set some money aside for once.

In his next letters, one just after Christmas and one on January 10, 1889, Will expressed delight at his father's and family's "kind words of encouragement and love" to Mattie and to him in their responses to his news. He said they were now planning a wedding in May, but could not be certain due to the unpredictable nature of his work. "Will send invitations, but hardly expect to see a great many of you."

*Lakme* was still not ready for sea, but its departure was just days away. The steamer was headed north to Seattle and Puget Sound ports for lumber to bring back to San Francisco.

One odd development at this time was an announcement in the *Daily Alta California*. On January 27, 1889, the newspaper ran a curious announcement, reporting the engagement of Mattie Graves and a William R. Bray, identified as "chief officer of the steamer *Lakme*"—which was Will Jackson's current assignment. Whether Will was using a fictitious name or a jealous suitor placed the notice remains a mystery.

—◦—

California, though possessing a mountainous coast, features four major harbors, San Diego, Monterey, San Francisco, and Humboldt Bay in the north. The state of Washington was blessed with the second largest in the country, Puget Sound.

The result of a complex estuarine system, including several rivers and four deep basins, Puget Sound is second only in size to Chesapeake Bay in the mid-Atlantic. Its waters flow from the Olympic and Cascade Mountains and the Sound spreads one hundred miles inland from the Pacific Ocean.

Mount Rainier—for which the ill-fated Sewall ship was named—rises 14,410 feet to the southeast, the fifth highest mountain in the continental United States.[1]

With timber as the most prolific resource in the post-Gold Rush era, fourteen lumber mills ringed Puget Sound. Sixty percent of the lumber that came to fast-growing San Francisco came from the heavily forested northern woods of the Pacific coast.

The steam schooner *Lakme* finally moved away from San Francisco on February 7, 1889. Its trip took no more than three weeks, making a quick round of several mills and returning with a full load of pine, Douglas fir, and other hardwoods. The steamer chugged through Port Townsend, Seattle, Tacoma, and Port Blakely in what Will described as "very cold weather" and, at one point, "a blinding snowstorm—seemed like home."

Will's account of the voyage came in a letter to his father Andrew on March 8, 1889, after "quite a nice trip." Writing from his room at the Graves home at 701 Shotwell Street on a rainy and stormy night, with Mattie sitting beside him and trying to get him to use capital I's rather than his preferred lower case i's, he was quite confident about his career prospects in addition to the upcoming wedding.

His major discovery on the voyage was the "incompetence" of the captain, a man named Harrison. "He is not the man to have there," he wrote home. "He is too old and not fresh enough."

The *Lakme's* owners, he reported, including Hinsdale, decided to give the captain one more chance—but assured Will that his own future was secure. "So, I am going to stop here until she gets back (from her next voyage), as I am confident he will be fired. If he does not, I'll have another place waiting for me, so I don't care much, in fact, I rather like it. As Mattie says, she can get ready to be married while I am ashore."

In fact, given this confidence and return to shore, Will and Mattie decided to move up their wedding date to mid-March.

He returned to the maneuvers over command of *Lakme*—or another vessel. He said he expected to get his captain's papers soon, "and make a hard push for a vessel" of his own. "It will be harder than it would be if I had money and plenty of friends behind my back, but it will be more to my credit if I make my point on my own resources."

He did have one key friend in his corner. The big news was that Will was scheduled to meet the very next day with Captain Hinsdale.

"Had quite a talk with Mr. Hinsdale yesterday. He told me to keep quiet and wait until the ship gets back. He says he is perfectly satisfied with me and will see me through, but the other owners put the Capt. there and they want to give him another trial."

Will went on to discuss preparations for the wedding, saying it might not be "a swell affair" and that he did not expect his father or his siblings to travel across the country, especially with such short notice.

"Am in hopes that I shall get along all right and see no reason why I should not make a success of this step in life. It gives me something to look ahead to and an objective in life."

On this evening, with many dramatic events and exploits well behind him, Will Jackson was a more mature, experienced young man. He now had a mentor and keen supporter, Captain Hinsdale, who was treating him like the son he never had. And this evening, March 8, 1889, Will was happy to tell his father he now expected to realize his long-time ambition—to be named a master, or captain, very soon. He was four months shy of his twenty-eighth birthday.

"I think if I don't get back in the steamer [*Lakme*] that Mr. Hinsdale will put me in charge of one of his schooners before long. Mr. Hinsdale told Captain Graves he would sooner have me captain of the steamer. But now if the other owners want to keep the current captain of the *Lakme*, they may put me in the schooner. I should prefer to be in the steamer, but of course I shall take the schooner if they offer her to me. *Am going down to the office tomorrow by appointment and have a talk with the owners.*"

Will then concluded his letter, noting that it was an unusually rainy evening in San Francisco, complete with thunder and lightning—"the first time I've ever heard it [here]."

"Well, Father, will finish tonight," he wrote. "Write soon, give love to all enquiring friends. Tell them to send all the Consolation they can. I expect to be a regular hen-pecked husband. Must not say too much as Mattie is looking at me. Well, at any rate, I am happy. So here goes with love from

Son Willis."

## Chapter Twenty-Two

# California and Drumm Streets

THE ORIGINS OF THE NAME OF DRUMM STREET, A FEW SHORT BLOCKS from the waterfront in San Francisco, are disputed, as is the background to the major street it intersects in the city by the bay, California Street.

Several historians say Drumm was named for Lieutenant Richard Coulter Drum, an army officer and veteran of the Mexican War first mentioned in fighting a fire on the Sacramento wharf in 1852. Others cite an army major, Andrew Drum, an Ohio farmboy who came to the city in the Gold Rush. Still a third attributes the name to an A. Drum who arrived on the ship *Tennessee* in 1850.

Lieutenant Drum's credentials survived the test of time in large part because he became the city's adjutant general during the Civil War, and later, after promotion to brigadier general, adjutant general of the United States Army.

The origins of the name California—and its application to one of the best known and longest streets in the city—are no more certain.

By all accounts, the name first appears on early maps of "downtown" San Francisco in 1839 when the city was still known as Yerba Buena ("Good Herb") and held no more than a few hundred residents. A survey ordered by the Mexican *alcalde* (mayor) placed the center of the city between California, Montgomery, Powell, and Broadway streets—today part of the boundaries of the financial district.

But first use of the name California is even more complicated than the background to Drumm. Research centers on both the use of the name in a sixteenth-century Spanish novel and a link to the Arabic word for leader, *caliph*, in an eleventh-century French epic poem, *The Song of Roland*.

Spanish explorers applied the name California to what they first thought was an island on the west coast—not a peninsula, Baja California, as it proved to be. They took the name from a long-admired novel written around 1500 by Garci Rodriguez de Montalvo, *Las Sergas de Esplandian*, a book about a land ruled by black Amazonian women whose leader was named Califia.

Not satisfied with that connection, historians have speculated that novelist Rodriguez de Montalvo was familiar with the fabled French poem in which Charlemagne muses about far off lands such as "Affrike" and "Califerne." Because the poem deals in part with Saracen warriors in the Middle East, the name of a place called Califerne was thought to have been derived from the Arabic word, *caliph*.

After an unusually stormy night, Will Jackson set out in the late morning of Saturday, March 9, 1889, to meet Captain Hinsdale to discuss his future and the latter's pledge to appoint him master of one of his vessels.

He walked from his room at Captain Graves's home on Shotwell Street in a light rain, southwest winds literally at his back as he headed toward the wharves to have lunch with his Bath friend Bamp Percy, an officer of the ship *Eli*, before going to Hinsdale's office.

Hinsdale was then general manager of the Pacific Pine Lumber Company, a successor to the Gardiner Mill Company, and owned a small fleet of steamers and schooners. Pacific Pine's offices were situated at 12 California Street, a stone's throw from the wharves.

Jackson and Hinsdale met at the corner of Drumm and California about 2:30 p.m., and then decided to walk to Pacific Pine's branch office at Pier 11, the likely location of the steamer *Lakme*, of which Will had been first mate on the voyage to Puget Sound.

Will was anxious to know Hinsdale's decision—to name him captain of the *Lakme* or the schooner *Zampa*. Either one would be fine, helping him to realize his life's ambition: master of a ship.

Hinsdale's decision will never be known.

As the two men walked across the intersection of Drumm and California streets, a runaway horse flew out of an alley and struck both men, hurling them ten to fifteen feet in the air.

Both men were knocked unconscious. Hinsdale fell on his face and was badly bruised. Will fell on the back of his head on the paving stones, incurring a severe concussion. In another of the bizarre coincidences of Will's young life, witnesses included a family friend and Maine native, Captain Warren Mills, and a man by the name of Charles Jackson. Mills and Charles Jackson picked both men up and started to render aid. Hinsdale soon recovered and was sent home. Charles Jackson, the son of a local sailmaker but no relation, and Mills, who knew Will Jackson but not where he lived, rushed him to San Francisco's Receiving Hospital, based at City Hall, about a mile and a half away.

Will Jackson never regained consciousness. After a fitful twenty-four hours, with Percy and another friend by his bedside trying to comfort him as he struggled to regain consciousness, he died at approximately 4:00 p.m. on Sunday, March 10. He was twenty-seven years, seven months old.

The cause was a severe hemorrhage and concussion of the brain.

Most of this information came from letters to Andrew Jackson from Will's good friend Bamp Percy, dated March 11, and another two days later from a Graves family relative, C.C. Dryden, who took it upon himself to organize everything from a post-mortem investigation to a funeral service to the shipment of Will's body to Bath, Maine. The Receiving Hospital went out of business years later, and many records were lost in the 1906 earthquake.

～～

On Monday, March 11, the *Daily Alta California* ran a brief news story headlined "Killed by a Runaway."

It read, with several mistakes: "C.W. Jackson, a seaman, who was knocked down by a runaway horse at the corner of Drumm and California streets on Saturday, died in the Receiving Hospital yesterday afternoon. Concussion of the brain was probably the cause of death.

"The remains were removed to the Morgue. Deceased was aged 30 [sic] years, and was a native of New York [sic]. Captain Hinsdale of the Pacific Pine Lumber Company, who was also injured by the runaway, is steadily recovering."

A brief death notice appeared in the *Daily Alta* and the *San Francisco Times* on March 13 with his correct name, origin (Bath, Maine), and age (twenty-seven).

The *Daily Alta* then followed up on March 15 with a more complete story on the tragic circumstances and Will Jackson's unfortunate fate.

Titled "A Sad Bereavement," it read: "R.W. Jackson, who died at the Receiving Hospital on Sunday last from the effects of injuries incurred by being knocked down on Saturday last by a runaway team, was chief officer of the steamer *Lakme*. He was a most estimable young man, and was to have been married early next month to Miss Mattie Graves, daughter of Sewell F. Graves, captain of the steamer *Point Arena*. His betrothed is completely overcome by her sudden bereavement. The remains of the young sailor have been sent East to the home of his childhood."

This account was the fullest and most accurate—except for suggesting the horse was part of a team of horses pulling a carriage. All subsequent reports and inquiries refer only to a single horse, dangling a loose harness.

———

Andrew Jackson was surely devastated by the news he received a day or two after the accident in a telegram from Will's friend Percy. No copy of the telegram survives.

A flood of correspondence and condolences arrived at 71 South Street in the following days. The first to arrive were the letters from Percy and Dryden—both expressing their deep sorrow but also providing as much information about the circumstances of the accident as they had been able to discover. Mattie Graves wrote several letters to Andrew pouring out her deep grief and affection for Will. Her mother, Amelia Batchelder Graves, also wrote. Dozens of relatives and family friends did so as well.

One common theme offered little consolation to Mr. Jackson and Will's brothers and sisters, but it did provide some reflection of Will's love of life and growing happiness at the moment that a bizarre fate befell him. It was best expressed by Percy, a fellow survivor of the wreck in the Marshall Islands, and Mrs. Graves.

After his expression of personal loss and details of the accident, Percy wrote: "I think the last few months of Will's life was very happy indeed, and he was in the best of spirits when he left me, little dreaming poor boy that it was the last time we would meet in this world. He and I have been like two brothers ever since we have been out here—no troubles one had that the other didn't know about."

Mrs. Graves commented: "We all loved your dear son. He was such a dear good boy. He endeared himself to everyone who knew him, and I am so thankful . . . that he was so happy the last few months of his life. It must be consoling to you to know that he had so many friends."

Mattie's mother also shared her daughter's reaction when she told her the news. "She could not shed a tear. I was afraid she would die. She could not have looked worse had she been dead. And now she is like a ghost. Her quiet grief worries me so, it nearly breaks our hearts to look at her."

Mattie did recover sufficiently to send several letters to the man she now regretted she could not call "Papa Jackson," as she had referred to him in talks about the future with Will.

"Dear Mr. Jackson: I didn't intend to write to you until I could call you father," she wrote in the first, a remarkably mature and articulate letter for a young woman of nineteen years of age. It was dated March 13, four days after the accident, three days after Will's death. "I cannot describe my feelings. If sympathy could only comfort us it would be a blessing. I don't know if I can finish this but I will try."

"Oh! How I wish I could walk in upon you and try and comfort you. Dear Will mailed a letter to you the morning he was hurt, telling you the change we had made"—to move up their marriage to March 21. "And now [that] will probably be the day of his funeral [in Bath]." She begged him to change it to another day, before or after the 21st. "It is all I can stand to think of the funeral being on any day, let alone our wedding day."

Mattie recalled that "Will was so *jolly* and in extra good spirits Saturday A.M. when he left the house [at Shotwell Street]. He seemed so happy all the time. I started out with him and he went as far as the grocery store with me where I ordered all of the material for our wedding cake. He was so pleased to think it was to be commenced."

In this and subsequent letters, she provided more details of their relationship and his having become a part of her family. "Mama loved him as much as if he were her own son; . . . Papa had so much interest in him (and his maritime career), and my sisters thought so much of their future brother." .

—— ~ ——

A funeral service, attended by a large number of friends, was held Thursday, March 14 at Porter's "undertaking parlors" on Eddy Street, according to a report in the *San Francisco Daily Call*. Reverend J.A. Cruzan of the Third Congregational Church presided, and part of the choir from his church sang several hymns.

> *After reading some passages from the Scriptures, Mr. Cruzan referred in feeling terms to the lamentable taking of the young life so full of promise and there were few dry eyes among those present as at its close the deceased's betrothed bent over the bier in uncontrollable grief and kissed the pallid lips of him who was to have been her partner and protector for life.*

The article concluded by describing Will Jackson as "a young man of fine promise" who had decided "to follow the sea from his fifteenth year." The article reviewed the drama of the wreck of the *Rainier*, his arrival in San Francisco and engagement to Mattie Graves.[1]

In the following weeks, Andrew Jackson did his best to seek more information about the accident, especially the owner of the horse. From three thousand miles away, he relied on two associates of Arthur Sewall, the Bath shipbuilder: his nephew, Oscar Sewall, and Andronicus Chesebrough, leading representatives of a major San Francisco shipping agency, Williams, Dimond and Co.[2]

At first, the horse's owner was said to be a Louis T. Snow, who owned a grocery and ship supply store at 210 California. Later reports back to Mr. Jackson identified the owner as a Thomas Benjamin Broderick, a delivery man and owner of three hauling carts who worked for Mr. Snow.

Arthur Sewall urged Mr. Jackson to press Oscar and "Andron" Chesebrough to contact a prominent San Francisco lawyer, Horace G. ("Major") Platt, and Oscar did write to Mr. Jackson on April 29 promising to do just that. But little apparently came of that inquiry.[3]

A coroner's inquest was held, according to Mr. Dryden. The *Daily Alta California* reported that "a coroner's jury brought in a verdict of accidental death" a few days after the accident.

Following the funeral service, Richard Willis Jackson's body left San Francisco by train at 8:00 p.m. Friday, March 15, 1889.

## CHAPTER TWENTY-THREE

# Homecoming

THE FRONT PAGE HEADLINE OF *THE BATH INDEPENDENT*'S WEEKEND EDI-
tion, March 16, 1889, delivered the sad news to the people of Bath and
the Kennebec River region.

### A BATH BOY KILLED.
#### Sad News by Wire from San Francisco
*After Many Hair Breadths Escapes on Sea He Meets a Violent
End on Land.*
*Remarkable Adventures on Sea and Land by a Smart Ken-
nebecker*
*His Boyhood's Accidents and Incidents—West Indian Cruises—
Wrecked on the Rainier—Exploits at Jaluit—Made King of Ujae—
In the Waves off Cape Horn—In the Northern Seas—An Officer of
the Largest Steamer Afloat—Incidents in the Life of Richard Willis
Jackson.*

The lead paragraph of the paper's article then said all one needed to know
about what had befallen Will Jackson: "Monday a telegram brought the
sad message that Sunday in San Francisco Richard W. Jackson of this city
was knocked down and killed by a runaway horse."

After providing details of the accident, its coming on the eve of Jackson's marriage to Ms. Graves and mentioning his young age, just a few
months shy of twenty-eight, the story continued: "Richard Willis Jackson
was a son of Andrew Jackson of this city, and during his early boyhood

was noted for his daring in athletic sports and the many narrow escapes he so often had."

The paper then offered a remarkably complete and detailed account of Will's life for the brief time it had to cover the story.

The article highlighted some of his adventures and exploits as an adolescent, including saving the life of a small boy from drowning, being struck by lightning, and various boating excursions. It recounted his courageous behavior as a young sailor during the wreck of the *Rainier* and survival in the Marshall Islands and his subsequent five years, many adventures, and steady promotions as a seaman based in San Francisco.

The article even speculated that Will—in character—may have been trying to halt the runaway horse when he was fatally injured.

"Mr. Jackson had great determination and was bound to succeed in spite of obstacles. He had an excellent education and ready wit. He was industrious and of good habits and, had he lived, would have been captain of a Pacific steamer before thirty years of age."

His career, it added, "by his own ability, is a testimonial of the young man's worth of which his family and friends may well be proud."

Suggesting all his exploits were "enough for a novel," it concluded: "After so much danger and adventure, when success seemed accomplished and happiness and wedded life were nearly attained by the gallant and brave sailor boy, his sudden death is a shock even to a stranger, and how much more so to his relatives, his promised bride and his many friends who knew him so long and so well. It is a sad, sad homecoming."

⎯ ⌣ ⎯

Will Jackson's embalmed body arrived in Bath that same day, March 16, and was taken directly to the family home at 71 South Street.

A funeral service for the young man was held the following Monday, March 18, at the house. Reverend Hanscom of the Wesley Methodist Church led the service, attended by many relatives and friends.

In the following weeks, Andrew Jackson continued to press Oscar Sewall and other agents on the West Coast for information and more details about the accident. But other than a determination that the runaway horse actually belonged not to the grocer Snow but to his cart hauler, Broderick, who apparently had left the horse unhitched to a post, no further evidence emerged.

The Register of Deaths of San Francisco City and County recorded Will's death as a "fracture of skull" after being struck by a horse. The incident contrasted sharply with most other deaths in San Francisco in early 1889; most others, many of them immigrants from China, Finland, and Norway, died as the result of gunshot wounds.

Visitors to the Jackson household in Bath continued to come for days and weeks following the funeral. Letters poured in as well.

Isaac R. Clark, a brother of Andrew's second wife, Annie Jones, wrote: "With unfeigned sadness, I hardly know how to give expression to my feelings in this sudden turn to your expectations. I am amazed as I read of the courage, bravery and self-possession always at his command, when no emergency deterred Richard Willis Jackson from attempting feats, however hazardous, to save life of others or to preserve himself from imminent peril.

"With your wife, our sister Annie, and [her sister] Edwina, whose relations bring them in close alliance, and to whom this event has caused most painful emotions, our family joins with united and earnest sympathy."

In later letters, Mattie Graves exchanged photographs with Mr. Jackson, and sent him some paintings of hers that she said Will had admired. And she informed him that they had found some money ($150) in Will's trunk they thought had been lost. A gold watch and collar button were lost in the accident, she added, though a chain for the watch was retrieved. The money helped defray the high costs ($600) of the undertaker's services and funeral.

Mattie discussed the possibility of accepting an invitation to travel to Bath and visit the Jacksons in a letter in early April. "I know if I could go I would have a nice time, and would feel perfectly content with Will's folks, and [be] where I could visit his grave whenever I wanted to." She also invited members of the Jackson family to come to San Francisco. "I wish Charlie would make up his mind and come out for a visit. We would welcome him just the same as if he were my brother. I imagine, from what I hear, that he is a great deal like Will was; if he is, we can't help loving him."

She added: "Will was such a favorite among his friends. And how happy I was to think that he chose me. And I was so proud of him. It seemed so strange to me that he didn't choose someone nearer his own age. He was just eight years older than I; his birthday comes the day before mine. It seemed so funny that our birthdays should come so near to each other."[1]

In a May 5, 1889, letter, Mattie reported she had planned to accompany her father on his next voyage, but his new vessel, a steamer, did not carry passengers. Captain Graves had been named master of *Lakme,* the steam schooner Captain Hinsdale had indicated he would offer to Will Jackson on that fateful day.

# Epilogue: Will Jackson Day

Richard Matthews Hallet, son of Will Jackson's younger sister, Alice, covered the last years of World War II in the Pacific for newspapers in his native Maine. Having grown up with stories of the exotic adventures and narrow escapes of his uncle Will, it was perhaps inevitable that he would find his way to the Marshall Islands as the war was winding down.

A Harvard-educated lawyer who had turned to writing as a career, by now an accomplished novelist and national magazine contributor, Hallet had followed his uncle's globe-wandering life in many respects. He had stoked coal on a transatlantic ship, dug for gold and cut timber in Canada, and hiked and canoed across Australia. Drawing on his experiences, he had written more than 150 short stories for leading magazines of the period and published five novels and an entertaining autobiography, *The Rolling World*. He once served on a British windjammer carrying oil to Sydney in hopes of setting foot on the atoll of Ujae where Will Jackson's ship *Rainier* had run aground in 1884.

"But adventure cannot be contracted for," he wrote in *The Saturday Evening Post* in its March 30, 1946, issue, in an article titled "My Uncle's Footprints." In the earlier venture, fresh out of law school in 1911, Hallet wrote: "I arrived in Sydney (124 days later) via the Cape of Good Hope without having been cast away at all or even faintly threatened with shipwreck."

But, thirty-six years later, as World War II was coming to an end, Hallet, working as a correspondent for Maine newspapers, told the story of Will Jackson and *Rainier*'s shipwreck to an influential US Navy admiral at Pearl Harbor, and with little fanfare the admiral arranged for Hallet to join a scheduled visit to the Marshall Islands by a team of doctors and educators.

"I had painted the picture of this Maine ship crashing down on that remote reef, the native outriggers swarming all around her, the ship's company looking dubiously at those wild fellows tumbling in the surf, with yellow flowers hanging from the holes in their ears." By the time Hallet and the American contingent made its visit in early June, 1945, US marines had captured the atoll and surrounding islands from the Japanese.

The following excerpts describe Hallet's visit to Ujae as related in *The Saturday Evening Post*, one of the most popular magazines of the era and one for which Hallet had written more than seventy short stories.

> *We entered [the oval lagoon] about noon through a break in the reef on the leeward side, and cast anchor about a mile offshore. Outriggers took us to the beach.*
>
> *It looked like a fatal blow to my prestige when it appeared that I must come ashore on the shoulders of a squat, muscular Marshallese, who stood chest-deep in water at the prow of the outrigger, and invited me to clasp my legs round his neck. Ensign Mike Rooney said I'd better do as I was told. The islanders would not think too highly of a white man who presented himself to them drenched to the skin, with his shins barked on coral.*
>
> *I, therefore, Will Jackson's nephew, came into Ujae piggy-back, and was dumped down on a coral beach of dazzling whiteness, lapped by a green sea and backed by tall palms. The natives of Ujae, 132 of them, were drawn up in a straight line from the water's edge up into the palms. With Rooney, I passed along this line like a political candidate, and shook hands with all—men, women, children and babies.*

Hallet then said he, Rooney, and an interpreter gathered the natives round them and he, Hallet, told them the story of the wreck of the *Rainier*, of the fortunes of the crew (including, no doubt, their kind treatment) and of their eventual rescue.

*I asked if any man or woman present was old enough to remember these events [his words turned into Marshallese by the interpreter].*

*There was a moment of silence. Then an old man, very shrunken, his eyes blue with incipient blindness, his bald head shining in the hot sun, stepped forward and spoke briefly.*

*"This is Lami," the interpreter told me. "He says that he was special boy to your uncle Will Jackson. He was told by the king to bring coconuts to his tent."*

*A great cry of surprise and joy went up from the natives. Their bare toes grasped excitedly at the coral pebbles.*

*"How big were you when you were my uncle's special boy," I asked Lami. The old man's fading eyes searched the crowd; then he put his withered hand on the head of a boy of twelve.*

*"I was as big as this boy. No bigger," he said.*

*As it was possible that old Lami was claiming acquaintance with Will Jackson merely to save me from disappointment, I tried to get him to say something positive, something that would check with my own knowledge.*

*"Can you remember the name of the captain's daughter?" I asked.*

*It was a thousand-to-one shot. Who would expect him to remember the name of that young white woman who had descended on him out of the struggling cloud of white canvas of a doomed ship pounding to pieces on the reef?*

*"Emma," he finally said.*

*Exactly so. It was Emma. Old Lami spoke the name with affection, as if she still lived warmly in his memory. There was a great stir, but old Lami, sunk in the past, only lowered his head and said "Emma, Emma," twice over.*

*"She was the age of this one," he added, getting up and putting his hand on the shoulder of a young woman of twenty-five whose black hair was stuck thick with yellow flowers.[1]*

Lami also told Hallet that the island spirit Libogen had predicted the wreck of a ship a day before the *Rainier's* accident. Reservedly, not wanting to insult his new interlocutor, Hallet asked him if Libogen was still "living in this island." Lami said no; a woman spirit, she had died when the previous king had died.[2]

Hallet then asked if there were any traces of the *Rainier*. He was told by Lami and others that the wooden wreckage was gone, but both pieces of iron and kerosene-soaked coral remained.

After being told where to find the remnants, Ensign Rooney, "rising to the occasion, cried: 'I proclaim tomorrow, June 9, a national holiday. Let this be known in Ujae as Will Jackson Day.'"

After a simple dinner and a night's rest, Hallet, Rooney, the interpreter, and a few others traveled down the lagoon to a place known as "Keerosin Ridge," after the *Rainier*'s cargo.

"Morning dawned with a fresh wind," Hallet wrote, "and our three outriggers slipped along like water skaters. The reef stretched away for twenty miles, a band of brilliant yellow. Beyond it was a band of tumbling surf whiter than any mortal pigment, and beyond that a band of blue sea."

Dodging a seven-foot shark the natives said was "friendly," they found several pieces of iron, clearly from *Rainier*, and salvaged a few, including one four-foot-long, V-shaped piece. They uncovered the bottom part of the ship's bell and the lower block of the lanyard rigging, and according to one report, were to return it to Bath.

A white crab with bright red markings scurried out from under one of the iron bars—"it was his tough luck to lose the house that had been made for him in Bath, Maine, sixty-odd years ago."

Upon their return, and following a time to rest, an "enormous" banquet was held at Government House. Many baskets were filled with coconuts, breadfruit, and boiled chickens, a luxury.

After the feast, Hallet continued, "25 or 30 girls came serpentining past our table. Their hair gleamed with coconut oil; their lips wore the friendliest of smiles, and they sang in stiff English their song of welcome."

"'Meester Hollot, we are very glad to see you; we kiss our lips to you,' they chanted in unison." Each of them offered a gift—a shell, a hardwood paper-cutter or a native fan.

"I thanked the women for their gifts and the men for their heavy exertions on the reef. I said their ancestors had been good to Will Jackson and his mates in their day of misfortune, and that they themselves now proved by their hospitality that their feelings for Americans were as kindly as in the old days. I expressed the profound hope that this historic occasion might not be forgotten, but rather that it would be handed down to their descendants as a bond between them and America."

Dances followed—some mild, some "wild" enough to send one of the islands' two preachers inside his house. The Marshallese then sang hymns taught them by Boston missionaries. "After a hasty conference, Rooney and I sang 'Old MacDonald Had a Farm.' They sang 'America,' and 'God Bless America,' and I responded with a chantey, 'Yankee Ship Comes Down the River.'"

After a prolonged exchange of good-night wishes, Government House emptied. "Rooney and I fell into our cots and slept like dead men. Will Jackson Day had been an immense and unqualified success."

The next day, Sunday, religious services were held, with two preachers presiding. Both men described "a heart line" [*to ene*] that stretches from friend to friend. They said they hoped that just as their lines had attached to Richard Hallet through his uncle and his engagement on the island sixty-one years ago, his heart line would attach to them in America "if they ever came to that strange land which has now taken the sovereignty of their Marshall atoll."

"Late that afternoon, I told the people of Ujae that a plane would come very soon and take me away. The words were hardly out of my mouth when a local official, who had been staring seaward, lifted his arm and cried: 'Balloon'—the native word for plane.

"All heads were lifted in amazement. How could I possibly know that the unseen plane would suddenly appear in the heavens?"

The official then leveled a finger at me and cried, "You—you—Meester Hollot—you Libogen!"

Of course, the plane's arrival was a bit of a coincidence. But Richard Hallet, who now knew well the supposed powers of the spirit, did not want to disillusion the official. "After all," he concluded his story, "I was Will Jackson's nephew, wasn't I?"

A second set of witnesses to the story of the *Rainier* and Hallet's visit can be found in a remarkable study of the people of the Marshall Islands by Jack A. Tobin, a researcher and writer who lived in the islands for more than three decades.

Tobin collected hundreds of stories and legends of the various tribes and incidents in the history of the island group in a 2002 book titled *Stories from the Marshall Islands.*

Several residents of Ujae recalled memories and traditions passed down by generations of "the American ship that drifted onto Ujae"— including annual celebrations of "Will Jackson Day."

With slight variations and intriguing details, the stories told to Mr. Tobin by several Ujaens confirm Richard Hallet's account in *The Saturday Evening Post.* Three of them remembered Hallet's visit at the end of World War II—though their name for him was "Allen, a naval officer," not Hallet, a correspondent. (Hallet did wear a naval officer's uniform during the visit, so the error is understandable).

A man by the name of Jelibar Jam, a former magistrate on Ujae and once an interpreter for Japanese rulers, recounted the story of the wreck of the *Rainier,* the reception of the people of Ujae, and the friendly interaction that developed between the "white men (and one woman) and the people of the atoll."[3]

Following retrieval of the goods from the ship, the initial meetings, and settlement, Jam recalled the story of "the American ship" and the details of the events that had been passed on from one generation to the next. A member of the Ejowa clan, sixty-one at the time he was interviewed by Tobin, Jam told him how the two leaders of Ujae, a Mr. Lakaien and a Mr. Lanibun, ordered the islanders to "take very good care of" the wreck's survivors. He said they exchanged goods, including food, and that the *Rainier's* crew taught the islanders how to put the kerosene to good use.

"The white men taught them how to make lamps with wicks and tins. And they did not extinguish them. The people of Ujae were very happy, and they took very good care of the white people."

In remembering Hallet's visit, which he witnessed personally at age thirty-one, Jam said that "Allen" came seeking the ship of his family that was wrecked there. He brought a "very old and small" book (*Wreck of the Rainier*) and asked questions about the names of the people on the ship.

Jam said Allen (Hallet) suggested the party and that both islanders and men on the naval ship prepared the food and all the crew joined the banquet on the second day of the visit. He said they played a game of baseball after the party and sang songs.

"When everything was finished, Allen said 'this is a day you will remember every year on the ninth of June. The name of this day is "Will Jackson's Day of Ujae."[4]

"And from that day to this," Jam added in his interview, "they do so (celebrate)."

Tobin attested to the account. "The fact that the story has been transmitted orally for generations, and that songs have been written about it, attest to this, as does the annual celebration of the event."

Tobin then noted that it was instructive to compare the preconceptions and attitudes of people from two different cultures and traditions, and excerpted a page from Omar Humphrey's *Wreck*—including the crew's initial fear of "savages" and preparations to load their guns.

Tobin observed that "the fears of the Americans were overcome by this friendly reception" and kind treatment before their rescue. He then noted that a séance by the spirit Libogen was mentioned by both Humphrey and the islanders.

Another resident, Enti Lucky, told Tobin a similar tale. He also said that the members of the *Rainier* had good reason to fear their reception after the shipwreck.

"The Marshallese people in previous times, times from long ago, killed all the castaways from ships that went adrift. But the people of Ujae did not."

Lucky remembered a song he'd heard as a boy, called "The White Men's Ship on Ujae."

> A ship over there, that ship that we have
> just seen and do not know what it is.
> That ship from the ocean.
> Moving from side to side

with the waves.
The ship is moving straight to
the rock, not to the pass. So that
the ship will be destroyed.
The wave on the reef is pushing
it toward the island. It is
taking it to the reef channel.

———

Peter Rudiak-Gould is one of the most recent Western visitors to provide an account of life on Ujae. In 2003, at the age of twenty-one, the new college graduate volunteered to teach English on the remote, mile-long Ujae island, the only inhabited islet of the kite-shaped, necklace-like Ujae atoll—two thousand miles from Honolulu, seventy miles from the nearest telephone, car, or store.

His book *Surviving Paradise* offers an entertaining and instructive portrait of the Marshallese inhabitants of Ujae at the turn of the twenty-first century, and the challenges of fate they have been dealt, as Rudiak-Gould notes, "from World War II battleground to (proximity to) American nuclear testing site(s) and imminent casualty of global warming."[5]

Rudiak-Gould's experience, of course, was far different than Will Jackson's. But his account provides a vivid chronicle of life on Ujae, which has an average elevation of seven feet about sea level, and by then 450 residents whose colorful language has eleven words for coconuts and thirty-three for different kinds of waves.

Framed by the immense gap between his romantic expectations of a tropical paradise and the realities of experience as a cultural orphan among friendly natives who spoke little English, living on a diet of bland rice and coconuts and watching old American films, the young teacher's report measures out as remarkably mature, witty, and honest.

Rudiak-Gould, a volunteer with World Teach, slowly became accustomed to the isolation of Ujae, smaller than many parking lots in his native California, with little more than a ten-minute walk separating the ocean side from the lagoon side of the islet. His sense of isolation is best captured in this observation—one that gives meaning to Will Jackson's long, wistful search for a sail on the horizon 120 years earlier.

Early in his ten-month assignment (one month longer than Jackson's stay on several islets), he wrote: "I found the highest point I could—a three-foot-tall dune—and scanned the horizon, but I couldn't see any other islands. There was only ocean in every direction. To the north, Bikini Atoll was invisibly distant at 150 miles. To the west, there was nothing until Ujelang Atoll, almost three hundred miles away. And to the south, the next stop would be one of the smallest countries in the world, Nauru, seven hundred miles away. Even Lae Atoll, thirty miles to the east, was hidden completely behind the curvature of the earth."[6]

His book—and personal recollections—do not include knowledge of the wreck of *Rainier* or a "Will Jackson Day." But he acknowledges that he may have simply not been aware of the celebration, in early June 2004, when he was getting ready to depart. He does recall being shown a coral reef called "*wod in karjeen*," which means kerosene coral, and told that this was the place where a sailing ship had been wrecked long ago and spilled kerosene. This was certainly the remains of the 1884 wreck.

Rudiak-Gould returned to Ujae three years after his volunteer work to examine the potential impact of global warming on the low-level islands as part of a master's degree thesis.

He noticed two distinct changes: the Marshallese had obtained more "stuff"—more lights, gadgets, DVDs of *Spiderman* and kick-boxing matches—and there were now scores of fallen trees and eroded shorelines. Higher tides were exposing ancient burial grounds.

"Whatever the cause," he wrote in the epilogue to his own book, "it made the threat of sea-level rise feel immediate and real, rather than distant and abstract." Some islanders also had heard about climate change and sea-level rise on the radio. Locals were sometimes concerned, other times complacent, pointing to the passage in Genesis in which God promises Noah that the Earth will never be flooded again.

A vivid portrait of Ujae, the adjoining islets, and the sprawling outcrops of rock and coral is best reflected in a description of the author's departure on one of Air Marshall Islands' planes.

"As we lifted into the sky, the world changed: The one-dimensional horizon opened into a living map. Huge expanses of reef passed by below and their colors were not the ones that should exist in the real world. A thousand shades of blue blended into a thousand shades of white. From the deep colors of the lagoon, the reefs rose to brilliant edges and barely submerged peaks.

"Every depth and underwater feature gave a different color to the sea. From underwater, coral reefs were the most alien landscapes I had seen on Earth; from the air, they were easily the most beautiful."

---

*Authors' note: At press time, a new survey by the World Bank projected that sea level rise poses an existential threat to the stability and existence of much of the Marshall Islands—one of only four atoll nations in the world. (The others: Kiribati and Tuvalu in the Pacific Ocean and the Maldives in the Indian Ocean).*

*A mere rise of one meter (approximately three feet) in sea level in this century could mean 40 percent of the buildings in the Marshall Islands capital of Majuro would be permanently flooded and entire islands and atolls could disappear, potentially costing the Pacific country its status as a nation.*

*The Marshalls, a country of 59,000 people which became independent from US trusteeship in 1986, is considered one of the countries most at risk due to climate change and the rise in sea levels. Atolls such as Ujae, home to approximately 364 people, could disappear in the event of more severe sea-level rise; the larger island of Jaluit is also certain to be at risk.*

*Under international law, statehood is established by stability, defined territory, and population. Adjustments such as reclamation of land, relocation of buildings, and shifts in population to higher islands and atolls may postpone the impact of the rise in sea level but flooding would continue to undermine stability.[7]*

*Also,* Blown to Hell: America's Deadly Betrayal of the Marshall Islanders, *a new book by Walter Pincus, documents the searing effects, contamination, and illnesses caused by sixty-seven nuclear tests conducted on Bikini and Enewetak, the northernmost atolls of the Marshalls, between 1946 and 1958. One test alone was one thousand times more explosive than the atomic bomb dropped on Hiroshima.*

# Acknowledgments

First and foremost, there is no one more important to the pub-lication of this book than the late Harriet Crooker Jackson Hill, my mother and Alexander's grandmother.

She had the wisdom and foresight to place the letters and a diary of her uncle, Richard Willis Jackson, in the hands of someone who would do his best to honor this young man's remarkable life story. It has taken a while, but I recall her saying, as she handed me Will Jackson's semi-legible, penciled, and fast-fading letters: "I'm sure you will find a good story in these."

Alex and I want to recognize several individuals who have been very generous and helpful in assistance to us in our research. Their deep knowledge of shipbuilding in Maine and California, their maritime acumen and careful reading of our text steered two landlubbers away from many mistakes and miscalculations in nautical matters and historic events. They include:

James Delgado, former director of the Vancouver Maritime Museum, Director of Maritime Heritage at the National Oceanic and Atmo-spheric Administration, and prolific author, historian and advocate of the maritime environment; James L. Nelson, acclaimed author of seafaring books ranging from American naval exploits during the Revolution and the War of 1812 to entertaining novels of Viking adventurers; Gina Bardi, reference librarian for the San Francisco Maritime National His-torical Park Research Center, in San Francisco; Dr. Charles Burden, a retired pediatrician and the individual most responsible for establishment of the Maine Maritime Museum, one of the leading nautical museums in the world; Ambassador Laurence E. Pope, distinguished diplomat, Middle East expert, and author of a number of books on topics ranging from American national security to French history; Robin A.S. Haynes, former manager of the Patten Free Library's Sagadahoc History and Genealogy Room in Bath, Maine, for her deep knowledge of the history of Bath; the Maine Maritime Museum in Bath, especially Nathan Lipfert, curator of the museum's excellent library for so many years, and other senior officials, notably Chris Timm and Kelly Page; the Bowdoin College Library and the college's outstanding Peary-MacMillan Arctic Museum, and its director, Susan A. Kaplan; Dale Greenley, chairman of the Douglas County (Oregon) Museum Advisory Board and Sylvia Rowan, librarian of the History Center of the San Francisco Library. Ms. Rowan and her colleagues searched for records of Will Jackson's accident and death in 1889 despite the loss of many records in the devastating 1906 earthquake. Also our thanks to Tom and Ash Kahrl, owners of the Bath Printing Company.

For other nautical and geographic/map advice, our appreciation goes to James Arsenault, one of the leading rare map and book dealers in North America; Christopher Boyle, a leading digital map expert; Neil Collins, General Manager of Derecktor Robinhood (Maine) Marine Center; Robin Nisbet, a Scottish professional photographer who lived on the remote Norfolk Island for 15 years; and David M. Brown, a writer and medicine man for all seasons who convinced us to retain Conrad's original use of "flick" of sunshine and not alter it to "flicker."

We also commend the amazing catalogue of articles and detailed information available from daily and weekly newspapers in California in the California Digital Newspaper Collection. This collection, provided by the University of California, Riverside, contains 17,616,451 articles at last count. It is available at https://cdnc.ucr.edu. They accept donations. Also, the *New York Times* archive and the Newspaper Archive (www .newspaperarchive.com) proved to be excellent resources for articles from the nineteenth century.

Several authors' work provided valuable background to the dynamic period of historic shipbuilding in Maine and the maritime life of San Francisco in the nineteenth century. Notably, they include *History of Bath,* by Henry W. Owen, and *A Maritime History of Bath, Maine and the Kennebec River Region,* by William Avery Baker. Among more recent books, we salute the outstanding history of the Sewall family of ship-builders produced by William H. Bunting, *Live Yankees*. Bill Bunting's book includes a concise account of the 1884 shipwreck in the Marshall Islands of *Rainier*, a Sewall ship, and the travails that set the stage for Will Jackson's remarkable—if short-lived—career. Bunting called Will Jackson "a smart young Mainer."

We benefited from the valuable firsthand witness of Peter Rudiak-Gould, a bold young Californian who like Will Jackson encountered challenges and adventure in the Marshall Islands—in his case by choice, not accident. At twenty-one, a year younger than Jackson at the time of his shipwreck on Ujae, Rudiak-Gould went to the tiny, mile-long island to teach English in 2003. His book *Surviving Paradise* offers an entertaining and instructive account of modern life on Ujae, and the spirit of a resilient people.

We salute the editors and production leaders at Rowman & Littefield's Lyons Press whose prowess and professionalism saw this work through brilliantly in the face of the pandemic, especially Rick Rinehart, editor, Tom McCarthy, and Lynn Zelem.

Our deep appreciation goes to Sarah Hill Schlenker, daughter and sister, whose careful, incisive editing was an essential step in completing this volume. We also thank her son Benjamin Schlenker, who at age nine, gave the first promotion of this book when he hosted the authors' presentation of an early draft before his fourth-grade class at Westchester Elementary in Catonsville, Maryland.

Lastly, to Marguerite Pooley Hill (Marty), wife, mother, and close companion, without whose enduring love, support, and technical skills with our computers and joint collaboration on different coasts of the continent—both bizarrely close to Will Jackson's origins and later life—this project could never have been completed.

Any errors or omissions are solely the responsibility of the authors.

# Appendix

## Will Jackson's Ships (1883-1889)

| Vessel | Year Built | Owner | Builder and Location | Type of Ship |
|---|---|---|---|---|
| *Jeanie* | 1883 | J. Winchester | Goss, Sawyer and Packard, Bath, ME | Schooner |
| *Rainier* | 1883 | A. Sewall & Co. | A. Sewall & Co., Bath, ME | Full-rigged ship |
| *W.F. Babcock* | 1882 | A. Sewall & Co. | A. Sewall & Co., Bath, ME | Fully-rigged ship |
| *Gatherer* | 1874 | Albert Hathorn | A. Hathorn, Bath, ME | Fully-rigged ship |
| *Karluk* | 1884 | | M. Turner, Benicia, CA | Brigantine (originally a whaler, became the flagship of the 1913 Canadian Arctic Expedition) |
| *Matthew Turner* | | Alaska CC | M. Turner, Benicia, CA | Schooner |
| *Maggie T. Morse* | | | | Schooner |
| *City of Topeka* | 1864 | Pacific Coast Steamship Company | Chester, PA | Passenger steamship |
| *Tropic Bird* | | John Kruse | Coos Bay, OR | Bark |
| *City of Peking* | 1874 | Pacific Mail Steamship Co. | John Roach & Sons | Passenger steamship |
| *Carlos Pacheco* | | Mexican International Line | Coastal schooner | Walter Colburn |
| *Zampa* | 1887 | George Hinsdale | Thomas Peterson, Port Madison, WA | Schooner |
| *Lakme* | 1888 | George Hinsdale | Thomas Peterson, Port Madison, WA | Steam schooner |

| Master | Dimensions | Will's Service | Position | Region |
|--------|-----------|----------------|----------|--------|
| A.C. Chaney | 800 tons, 186 feet | 1883 | Seaman | Coastal |
| Samuel Morrison | 1,877 tons; 233 ft. | May 1883– Jan.1884 | Seaman | Pacific |
| James Murphy | 2,028 tons, 241 ft. | Sept. 1884– June '85 | Boatswain | Atlantic & Pacific |
| J.S. Lowell | 1,509 tons, 208 ft. | July 1885 | Did not go | Atlantic & Pacific |
| | 247 tons, 129 ft. | 1886 | Mate/2nd mate | Alaska |
| | | 1887 | | |
| | 60 tons | 1887 | | West Coast |
| Rogers | 1,057 tons, 198 ft. | July 1887 | 3rd officer | So. California– Guatemala |
| Jackson | 172 tons | Dec. 1887 | "Prize Master" | San Diego–Mexico |
| | 5,079 tons, 423 ft. | Mar. 1888 | 4th officer | Asia |
| | | July 1888 | | Coast to Mexico |
| Harrison | 322 tons | Late 1888 | 1st mate | Puget Sound |
| | 529 tons, 171 ft. | 1888–89 | 1st mate | Alaska |

# Sources and Notes

**Preface**
1. Joseph Conrad, *The Nigger of the Narcissus*, 99.

**Chapter One**
1. Simon Winchester, *Pacific*, 2

**Chapter Two**
1. Historical references to the Crooker family, the history of Bath and its once-dominant shipbuilding industry in this chapter and others are taken from a number of texts, including Henry Owen, *History of Bath* (1936), William Avery Baker, *A Maritime History of Bath, Maine and the Kennebec River Region* (1973), William H. Bunting, *Live Yankees* (2009), and Frederic B. Hill, *Ships, Swindlers and Scalded Hogs* (2016).
2. *Bath Times*, May 17, 1927; Article in series "Ye Good Olde Days," as related by Charles T. Jackson, brother of Will Jackson.

**Chapter Three**
1. Timothy G. Lynch; *Beyond the Golden Gate*, 2015.
2. *Maritime Notes and Queries, from A Record of Shipping Law and Usage, Vol. 3.* Edited by Sir William Mitchell, 1875.
3. John E. Duncan, *The Sea Chain*. (Scotia, N.Y., Americana Review, 1986). Charles Crooker Duncan later became Commissioner of the Port of New York and fared badly in a bitter and protracted dispute with Mark Twain, who reported in New York's leading newspapers on how Duncan had placed three of his sons on the city payroll at double and triple the salaries of other employees. Old antagonists, Twain had written his first major best-seller, *Innocents Abroad*, on a voyage to Europe on a ship, *Quaker City*, captained by Duncan. For a more complete account, see Hill, *Ships, Swindlers and Scalded Hogs*, 225.
4. The party, which drew its name from members' denial of belonging to it by saying "I know nothing," became the American Party in 1855 and eventually was absorbed by the Republican Party a few years later.

5. See Richard White's *The Republic for Which It Stands,* Oxford University Press (2017) for a superb account of the period of Reconstruction and the Gilded Age. Also, Gale's *American Eras: Primary Sources. Business and the Economy: Vol. 8, Development of the Industrial United States, 1878-1899.* U.S. History in Context. 1997, pp. 93-95.

6. For an excellent account of Garfield's election and botched treatment, see Candice Millard, *Destiny of the Republic; A Tale of Madness, Medicine and the Murder of a President.*

7. *Bath Daily Times,* March 2, 1883; 3.

8. Diary of Charles T. Jackson.

## CHAPTER FOUR

1. Baker, *A Maritime History,* 526.

2. US Report on Commerce and Navigation for 1854.

3. References to the Sewall shipyard are taken largely from William H. Bunting, *Live Yankees; The Sewalls and Their Ships,* 2009.

4. Guy C. Goss had earned his maritime stripes the old-fashioned way—going to sea while still in his teens, working his way up the nautical ladder, and assuming his first command at age thirty, a brig, *Florence Nightingale,* from Boston. He sailed the world for another decade until the illness of his children called him home. His last command came in 1862, whereupon he settled in Bath. Development of schooners, brigs and full-rigged ships followed not long after, spurred by his partnering with another Maine native, Elijah Sawyer.

5. Hyde was a remarkable leader who saw the need to build local industry—in part to retain the young people of the region. On his inauguration for a second term as mayor in 1881, he warned of a grave trend that still haunts the state of Maine in the twenty-first century: 'We carefully educate and train our young men to a certain point, when they are compelled in large measure to give the vigor of the best part of their days to building up other sections and places."

6. Harry "Bamp" Percy, a friend of Jackson's, was third officer, and about the same age as Jackson.

7. By 1911, the state of California was the world's greatest oil-producing region, accounting for 63 per cent of US production. Lynch, *Beyond the Golden Gate,* 2000.

## CHAPTER FIVE

1. The distance in 2019, transiting the Panama Canal, sailing west, is approximately 10,200 nautical miles, according to several shipping companies.

2. Oddly, the weekly *Bath Independent* reported in its "Society Gossip" column of May 12 that "Andrew Jackson today is united in marriage to a Thomaston lady of wealth," without any further information that day or in subsequent editions. Local papers, like many across the country, often were filled with unsubstantiated gossip. The vital records of the city of Thomaston, however, do list their marriage in Warren, Maine, near Thomaston, on that date.

3. Simon Winchester, *Krakatoa,* 2003.

4. Indonesia's tectonic plates and subduction zones have produced more volcanoes than any other single country, eighty-seven; and three of the five worst volcanic eruptions in history occurred there. See Winchester, *Krakatoa*, 307.

Winchester's book delves deeply into the origins of volcanic eruptions around the world, providing fascinating background ranging from ancient legends and religious beliefs to the modern discovery of "plate tectonics" and continental drift. "Here was the event that presaged all the debates that continue to this day about global warming, greenhouse gases, acid rain and ecological interdependence." Winchester, *Krakatoa*, 269.

## CHAPTER SIX

1. William H. Bunting, *Live Yankees*, 191.
2. Richard Henry Dana Jr., *Two Years Before the Mast*. Dana was fortunate to be able to get away from Thompson when a new captain, Edward Horatio Faucon, a highly regarded master, took over *Pilgrim* for its return to the East Coast.
3. Many years later, a Sewall relative described Emma as "a harum-scarum girl, good fun, with light hair and freckles—with plenty of courage" in Bunting, *Live Yankees*.
4. William H. Bunting, *Live Yankees*, 192.
5. Frederick C. Matthews, *American Merchant Ships, 1850–1900*.

## CHAPTER SEVEN

1. Descriptions of Norfolk Island and the experiences of *Rainier*'s crew come from Jackson's letters home, his articles in the *Bath Independent* and the book *Wreck of the Rainier* by Omar H. Humphrey (and, in part, Will Jackson).
2. Australia assumed direct governance of Norfolk Island in 2015 after many decades as a self-governing Australian state.
3. *An Early American Voyage to the Isles of the South Seas*, by Donald Mackay; unpublished journal; James Arsenault and Company, Arrowsic, Maine.
4. The famous voyage and mutiny of HMS *Bounty* occurred in April 1789, when master's mate Christian Fletcher and twenty-five other seamen took over command of the ship near the island of Tonga. Captain William Bligh and eighteen loyalists were set adrift in a twenty-three-foot open launch in the middle of the Pacific with the expectation they would not survive. Miraculously, Bligh and his men did survive, were eventually rescued, and were returned to England. After unsuccessful efforts at settlements on various islands, Fletcher, a smaller number of fellow mutineers, and Tahitian men and women finally settled on Pitcairn Island in January 1790, more than 1,000 miles east of Tahiti. They built a community which by 1855 had grown to just under 200 descendants of the original settlers. The island could not sustain their growing population so with the approval of the British Government the residents then embarked on a journey to Norfolk on May 3, 1856.
5. Not a known title, B.B. probably stands for Bath Boy, a common reference in Bath newspapers to sailors from Bath, and the C.S. to Chief Steward. Jackson had become the steward by this point.

## CHAPTER EIGHT

1. In marine terminology, "dog watch" referred to the four hours between 1600 and 2000 that on ships at sea were split into two two-hour shifts of two hours each to facilitate the division of watches among officers and crew, and to allow for dinner.
2. The easternmost islands of Micronesia, the Marshalls came under the control of many nations over the centuries, from early Spanish and Portuguese influence to Russia, Germany, Japan, and, after World War II, the United States. It became an independent nation in 1986.
3. This account and further descriptions of the wreck are related in Humphrey's *Wreck of the Rainier* and Jackson's diary and letters.
4. William H. Bunting, *Live Yankees*, 194.

## CHAPTER NINE

1. Frederick C. Matthews, *American Merchant Ships* (1850–1900), 254.
2. Humphrey, in his book, revealed that the "king" was named Elijah Bullock, but did not provide any more background.
3. Jackson's diary of the voyage from Philadelphia provided confirmation, more briefly, of Humphrey's account in the published book.

## CHAPTER TEN

1. "The Story of a Ship," by Harry Whalen Drohan, *Galveston Times* (about 1892).
2. The behavior of the natives is covered extensively in Humphrey's *Wreck of the Rainier* and Jackson's letters and newspaper articles.

## CHAPTER ELEVEN

1. US Consular records show that a small consular office on Jaluit was manned by a F. Pfeffer, of unknown nationality, from late 1883 until 1886. No other records survive. *The Diplomat's Dictionary*, by Amb. Chas. W. Freeman, Jr., reports that a consul was "not always a native of his host state, and his work is usually part-time." A consul is supposed to provide "non-discriminatory treatment for their nationals" in all problems and "arrange for their repatriation." Pfeffer offered virtually zero assistance to survivors of the shipwreck.
2. The term "kanaka" was liberally used to indicate a native of the South Sea islands. Thousands of natives, often called kanakas, were employed as slaves on Australian cotton and sugar plantations in the late nineteenth and early twentieth centuries, and, considered good sailors, were recruited by whaling ships in the Pacific.
3. This USS *Essex* was one of the most heralded warships of the US Navy at the time, the third by that name. Built in Boston in 1876, the 185-foot, 1,375-ton screw steamship was in the midst of a 52,648-mile circumnavigation of the globe when it received orders to go to the Marshalls to rescue the officers and crew of *Rainier*. The *Essex* eventually came back to New York in late December 1884 after thirty-eight months at sea. (*New York Times* archive, December 31, 1884, 8.) Records show that Commander

McCormick had rewarded the natives on Jaluit with gifts of axes, a hand saw, fishing gear, and large amounts of rice and bread.

## CHAPTER TWELVE

1. Omar H. Humphrey, *Wreck of the Rainier*, 138.
2. Several years later, Drohan wrote a long and detailed article of the *Rainier*'s voyage and his own travails in a Galveston, Texas, newspaper. Headlined "The Story of a Ship," he wrote that he and his crew were at wit's end three weeks after leaving Ujae, with no more than a bit of meat and two biscuits left, when they spotted possible land (probably Strong's Island in the Solomon Sea) and what looked like a canoe almost at the same moment. The "canoe" turned out to be the *Catalina* and Drohan raised the makeshift flag made by Emma Humphrey. When the English captain shouted "What boat is that?" Drohan replied: "The American ship *Rainier*'s longboat, cast away on the Marshall group, January 2, 1884."
3. Omar H. Humphrey, *Wreck of the Rainier*, 140.
4. Captain Morrison's official account differed little from his initial report to Arthur Sewall of "the total loss" of *Rainier*. Filed with and signed by Consul General Thomas B. Van Buren, the protest said "on January 2, 1884, at 9:30 p.m, the ship ran on to a half-tide coral reef it being a dark and hazy horizon could not see it in time for ship to answer helm. Soon after came on squally wind and sea increasing, ship rising and falling with destructive force, until about noon next day ship bilged and went on to her beam ends with a list off shore." Morrison, defensively, again stated that the reef and atoll were not "laid down on my charts." Marine Extended Protest of Ship *Rainier*, in port of Kanagawa (Yokohama) Japan, May 15, 1884.
5. See *When Copra was King: A Micronesian Seminar Photo Album*, by Hezel, S.J. and Berg, M.L.
6. Omar H. Humphrey, *Wreck of the Rainier*, 77 (Jackson part).
7. Omar H. Humphrey, *Wreck of the Rainier*, 78 (Jackson part).

## CHAPTER THIRTEEN

1. *Bath Independent*, March 16, 1889.
2. Frederick C. Matthews, American Merchant Ships (1850–1900); 346. The *Babcock*, which was considered one of the fastest vessels on the long runs around Cape Horn, survived several mishaps during a near four-decade career. The ship was acquired by the US Navy in 1917 and operated as a collier until the end of World War I.
3. Thomas G. Lynch, *Beyond the Golden Gate*, 133.
4. William H. Bunting, *Live Yankees*, 287.
5. Captain Murphy left the *Babcock* in 1889 to oversee completion and take command of another Sewall ship, *Shenandoah*, a four-masted barque regarded as one of the most majestic ships of the late nineteenth century. At 299.7 feet and 3,258 tons, she was also the largest wooden ship ever built at that point—yet regarded as easy to handle.
6. Sewall Family Papers, 1761–1965. Box 529, Folder 15. Maine Maritime Museum, Bath, Maine.

7. See Chapter 3 for more detailed background on this disreputable practice.

8. The first significant absentee voting occurred for soldiers during the Civil War, but most states did not adopt the practice until the early 1900s.

9. William Avery Baker, *A Maritime History*, 653.

10. Review by Jonathan Dore, for The *Times Literary Supplement*, of *Rounding the Horn: A Deck's-Eye View of Cape Horn*, by Dallas Murphy (Basic Books, 2015).

11. For a detailed account of the wreck and a prolonged rescue of *Oracle's* officers and crew, see Frederick C. Matthews' *American Merchant Ships* (1850–1900); pages 222–227.

12. Sewall Family Papers. Box 529, Folder 16. Maine Maritime Museum. Bath, Maine.

## CHAPTER FOURTEEN

1. Sewall files show that the US consul in Hong Kong arranged an auction of *Rainier's* longboat, and, after fees, returned $85.50 of the $95 offer to the Sewalls. Second mate Drohan claimed he donated the boat to the captain of *Catalina*. Sewall Family Papers. Collection 22, Box 417, Folders 18 and 19; Maine Maritime Museum, Bath, Maine.

2. Many abandoned Gold Rush ships were scuttled and became part of the waterfront foundation of San Francisco. The bones of the *William Gray* were excavated in the 1980s and placed on the National Register of Historic Places. For more information; see *Ships, Swindlers and Scalded Hogs: The Rise and Fall of the Crooker Shipyard in Bath, Maine* (Down East Books, 2016), by the author, and *Gold Rush Port: The Maritime Archeology of San Francisco's Waterfront*, by James P. Delgado, (University of California Press, 2009).

## CHAPTER FIFTEEN

1. Thomas G. Lynch, *Beyond the Golden Gate*, 43. Lynch's book provides an excellent review of sixteenth- to eighteenth-century exploration of the west coast of North America, including the odd but repeated failure of Spanish expeditions to discover the opening to San Francisco bay.

2. William Issel and Robert W. Cherny, *San Francisco, 1865–1932*, 16.

3. James P. Delgado, *Gold Rush Port*, 7

4. By late 2019, California's economy, slightly more than $3 trillion, was the fifth largest in the world in terms of gross domestic product, stronger than that of India, France, the United Kingdom, South Korea, Brazil, etc.—and twice as large as Russia, which ranks twelfth. See International Monetary Fund. https://www.imf.org/external/datamapper/NGDPD@WEO/OEMDC/ADVEC/WEOWORLD

5. Dozens of other stanzas show up in various records—including "What was your name in New York, was it Clancy, O'Toole or O'Rourke?" It was a popular song, adapted by Johnny Mercer, in the 1963 film *How the West Was Won*. Some historians trace its most common use, if not its origins, to the Gold Rush era.

6. William Avery Baker, *A Maritime History*, 521.

7. *New York Times*, August 25, 1906, 7

8. *Daily Alta California*, April 5, 1882.

9. Basil Lubbock, *The Downeasters*, 92

10. Seaman's Friend, Volumes 53–54. Year, *Sacramento Daily Union*, March 16, 1882, and *Daily Alta California*, February 27, 1884.
11. Curtis died of consumption in prison in April 1884. Captain Sparks died of delirium tremens in San Francisco in 1896, according to a 1906 *New York Times* article. Another report said he committed suicide by jumping off another ship, *Red Cross*, in mid-ocean, December 1884. Watts, who eventually died a violent death in a logging camp, was pardoned by President Grover Cleveland, July 13, 1886, after a strenuous lobbying campaign by his original defense lawyer, who claimed the sailors made up their stories of abuse and torture. From *Daily Alta California*, July 13, 1886.

## CHAPTER SIXTEEN

1. William Avery Baker, *A Maritime History*, 612.
2. The 129-foot, 247-ton brigantine *Karluk* enjoyed a long career in Alaskan waters, mainly as a whaling and salmon fishing vessel. Despite its relatively small size and age, it was chosen in 1913 as the flagship of the ill-starred Canadian Arctic Expedition by its leader, Vilhjalmer Stefansson.

Captained by a respected master, Robert A. Bartlett, the armor-plated *Karluk* became stranded in an early ice pack off the north coast of Alaska in August, 1913. Stefansson and several colleagues left the ship soon afterwards to go caribou hunting—and abandoned efforts to find it when they returned.

*Karluk* floated with the moving ice for up to four months, with Bartlett and crew constantly off-loading—and reloading—food and supplies in case the ship sank. The ship finally did fall beneath the Arctic ice on January 11, 1914, with Bartlett staying on board to the very last minute, drinking coffee and tea and playing Chopin's Funeral March on the ship's Victrola. Under Bartlett's leadership, aided by the hunting and survival skills of his Inupiat guides, the remaining crew made their way to Wrangel Island—a large, whale-shaped island north of Siberia. As many as eleven of the remaining crew perished during the ordeal, from disease, a suicide, and unwise decisions.

Bartlett and a young Inupiat hunter, Kataktovik, walked across seven hundred miles of ice from Wrangel to Siberia and sent a wireless message that led to the rescue, seven months later, of the remaining twelve crew members.

Sources: "Defying the Ice: Shipwreck and Rescue of the *Karluk*." Exhibit of the 1913 Canadian Arctic Expedition; Peary-MacMillan Arctic Museum, Bowdoin College, Brunswick, Maine (2016); and *The Last Voyage of the Karluk*, by William Laird McKinlay. New York: St Martin's Griffin, 1976.

## CHAPTER SEVENTEEN

1. See Michael Sims' *Arthur and Sherlock* for a fascinating account of the writing life of A. Conan Doyle, an Edinburgh doctor who turned to writing popular detective novels. *Beeton's Christmas Annual*, a popular magazine in the United Kingdom between 1860 and 1898, was the first British firm to publish Harriet Beecher Stowe's *Uncle Tom's Cabin*.

2. Few copies of *Wreck* have survived. They are not so rare as to be a collector's item, but one book store in Australia advertised a copy of the hardback for $1,000 several years ago.

## CHAPTER EIGHTEEN

1. Later legal proceedings revealed that the usual captain of *Tropic Bird* was a crusty and infamous seadog, George Caleb. Caleb had been imprisoned several years earlier by Mexican authorities over a disputed manifest, and apparently decided not to enter Mexican waters again, thereby turning over command of *Tropic Bird* before reaching Ensenada with a cargo of lumber from Eureka, California. Owners of the *City of Topeka* won $600 for salvage of *Tropic Bird* in legal proceedings.

2. *City of Topeka* had a long and colorful career as both a freight and passenger vessel. It took passengers between Washington State, mainly Seattle and Puget Sound, and Alaska for many years, especially during the Yukon Gold Rush (1896–1899). It was badly damaged on a submerged rock off Wrangell Narrows, Alaska, in March 1899. And it was one of the three ships sent in January 1906 to try to rescue survivors of the sinking *SS Valencia*, a former Spanish-American War troopship that ran aground in foul weather off the treacherous southwest coast of Victoria Island. One-hundred and thirty-six people perished, thirty-seven were rescued, in what was considered "the worst maritime disaster" in the "graveyard of the Pacific," as that area of British Columbia was known.

3. Making 116 round trips between San Francisco and the ports of Yokohama and Hong Kong between 1875 and 1903, *City of Peking* brought thousands of Japanese and Chinese immigrants to the United States. *City of Tokyo* did not fare well: It was destroyed off the coast of Japan in a typhoon in 1885.

## CHAPTER NINETEEN

1. William Fairburn, *Merchant Sail*, 3201.

2. In a sign of the times, and growing interest in the world, thirty-three scholars, scientists and explorers founded the National Geographic Society on January 13, 1888, in Washington to encourage exploration of the globe.

3. Captain Edgar "Ned" Wakeman had died before Jackson's time in the West, in 1875. He was the epitome of a crusty old salt who had gone to sea at twelve, lived through various adventures, and became a ship captain—"tattooed from head to foot like a feegee, a Fiji Islander," wrote Mark Twain. Twain had traveled on a Wakeman ship in 1866 and based the character of Captain Ned Blakely, the protagonist in his first book, a semiautobiographical travelogue, *Roughing It*, on Wakeman. Jackson, who recommended Wakeman's memoir to his family, would come to know his son, Edgar L. Wakeman, about his age, an author himself.

## CHAPTER TWENTY

1. *The Klamath Exploring Expedition*, 1850; Oregon Historical Society, December, 1916; pp. 341-357.

2. "The Gardiner That Was," Georgina Durbin, Douglas County Historical Society, 2011; reprint of a 1969 article in the *Umpqua Trapper*.
3. *Descendants of Robert Hinsdale, of Dedham, Medfield, Hadley and Deerfield*; edited by Alfred L. Holman, Lombard, Illinois, 1906; 592.

## CHAPTER TWENTY-ONE

1. The mountain itself has had several names, but the US Park Service finally made Rainier official in 1890. British explorer George Vancouver originally named it for a naval colleague, Rear Admiral Peter Rainier.

## CHAPTER TWENTY-TWO

1. *San Francisco Daily Call*, March 15, 1889, as republished in the *Bath Independent* of March 30, 1889.
2. Mr. Chesebrough, a native of Baltimore, had become a close ally of Arthur Sewall and steered a good deal of business toward Sewall ships. Among other hugely profitable enterprises, Williams and Dimond controlled the Hawaiian sugar trade and operations with the Santa Fe and Mexican Central railroads. In a weird coincidence, one of the many that shadowed Will Jackson's life, a Sewall ship *Chesebrough* (launched in Bath in 1878) sank during a typhoon off the far northwest coast of Japan in October 1889, after delivering a cargo of kerosene to Hiogo (Kobe)—the same destination of the ill-fated *Rainier* five years before, carrying a similar cargo and just seven months after Jackson's death in San Francisco.

Following repairs from the early days of the typhoon, the 1,500-ton ship was returning to New York with a cargo of sulfur when it lost several sails and ran aground in heavy seas near the village of Shariki. All but four of the twenty-three on board drowned, including the captain, Peter Erickson, a resident of Bath, as were several other members of the crew. Residents of Shariki who helped rescue the survivors built a monument to the dead, holding observances on the anniversary of the accident even through World War II.

Officials of the community of Tsugaru City, later formed by residents of Shariki and other small villages, contacted Bath city officials in 1989 on the hundredth anniversary, and a sister-city relationship was formed in 1990—an organization that thrives to this day with annual exchanges of students and parents each year.
3. Platt was the right man to go to if anything could be done. One of the most respected attorneys in the city, a Democrat and later a Republican political leader, Platt was known as the most eloquent orator on the west coast. Obituary, *San Francisco Call*, August 30, 1910.

## CHAPTER TWENTY-THREE

1. Mattie Graves did marry the following year, to Edward P. Bemis, a Massachusetts native, and they had four children. 1900 Census, Alameda, California.

# Epilogue

1. Emma Morrison Humphrey had been only slightly younger, probably 22, in 1884.
2. Richard M. Hallet article, *Portland (Maine) Press Herald,* June 10, 1945.
3. Jack A. Tobin, *Stories from the Marshall Islands,* 359.
4. Jack A. Tobin, *Stories from the Marshall Islands,* 361.
5. Sixty-seven nuclear tests were carried out on Bikini and Eniwetok atolls in the Marshall Islands by the United States after the end of World War II, most many times more explosive than the atomic bomb dropped on Hiroshima. Many residents suffered illnesses attributed to radiation, but a suit against the US and other nuclear powers, citing those illnesses and alleged failure to observe international disarmament obligations, was narrowly rejected in October 2016 by the United Nations' highest court.
6. Peter Rudiak-Gould, *Surviving Paradise,* 12.
7. World Bank survey: "Adapting to Rising Sea Levels in Marshall Islands." https://storymaps.arcgis.com/stories/8c715dcc5781421ebff46f35ef34a04d. Accessed October 22, 2021.

# BIBLIOGRAPHY

Albion, Richard Greenhalgh. *The Rise of New York Port (1815–1860)*. New York: Charles Scribner's Sons, 1939.

Aldridge, Richard. *Memories of Morse: A 75th Anniversary Tribute to Morse High School (1904–1979)*. Brunswick, ME: Brunswick Publishing Company, 1979.

Baker, William Avery. *A Maritime History of Bath, Maine and the Kennebec River Region* (two vols.). Bath, ME: Marine Research Society of Bath, 1973.

Beckham, Stephen Dow. *Land of the Umpqua: A History of Douglas County, Oregon*. Roseburg, OR: Douglas County Commissioners, 1986.

Bunting, William H. *Live Yankees: The Sewalls and Their Ships*. Gardiner, ME: Tilbury House; and Bath, ME: Maine Maritime Museum, 2009.

Caldwell, Bill. *Rivers of Fortune: Where Maine Tides and Money Flowed*. Portland, ME: Guy Gannett Company, 1983.

Cary, Richard. *Richard Matthews Hallet: Architect of the Dream*. Waterville, ME: Colby College Quarterly 7, No. 10: 416–452 (June, 1967).

Chapman, William. *Sketches of Nineteenth Century Whitewash Civilization*. 1895. (Harvard College Library Sheldon Fund).

Conrad, Joseph. *Youth, A Narrative, and Two Other Stories*. London: Blackwood and Sons, 1902. (Originally published as *Youth*, in *Blackwood's Magazine*, 1898).

———. *The Nigger of the Narcissus*. New York: Harper Brothers, 1951. (Original publication: New York: Doubleday and Company, 1897).

Corman, Edwin T., and Helen M. Gibbs. *Time, Tide and Timber: A Century of Pope and Talbot*. Palo Alto, CA: Stanford University Press, 1949.

Dana, Richard Henry, Jr. *Two Years Before the Mast: A Personal Narrative of Life at Sea*. Los Angeles: The Ward Ritchie Press, 1964. (Original publication: New York: Harper and Brothers, 1840.)

Delgado, James P. *Gold Rush Port; The Maritime Archaeology of San Francisco's Waterfront*. Berkeley: University of California Press, 2009.

Duncan, John E. *The Sea Chain*. Scotia, NY: American Review, 1986.

Fairburn, William. *Merchant Sail* (Vols. 1–6). Center Lovell, ME: Fairburn Marine Educational Foundation, 1947.

Freeman (Ambassador), Charles W., Jr. *The Diplomat's Dictionary*. Washington: National Defense University Press, 1994.

Hallet, Richard Matthews. "My Uncle's Footprints." *Saturday Evening Post*, March 30, 1946.

Hebberer, H. Miles. *History of Williams, Dimond and Company* (1862–1962). San Francisco: 1962. Collection of San Francisco Maritime National Historical Park.

Hezel, Francis X., and M.L. Berg. *Micronesia: Winds of Change.* Trust Territory of the Pacific Islands, 1995.

Hill, Frederic B. *Ships, Swindlers and Scalded Hogs: The Rise and Fall of the Crooker Shipyard in Bath, Maine.* Rockport, ME: Down East Books, 2016.

Hill, Frederic B., and Alexander Jackson Hill. *The Correspondence of Richard Willis Jackson: A Seaman's Journey Around the World.* Unpublished manuscript, 1997.

Humphrey, Omar J. *Wreck of the Rainier.* Portland, ME: W.H. Stevens, 1887.

Issel, William, and Robert W. Cherny. *San Francisco 1865–1932: Power, Politics and Urban Development.* Berkeley: University of California Press, 1986.

Jasanoff, Maya. *The Dawn Watch: Joseph Conrad in a Global World.* New York: Penguin Random House, 2017.

Jean-Aubry, Georges. *Joseph Conrad: Life and Letters* (two vols.). Garden City: Doubleday and Page, 1927.

Judd, Richard W., Edwin A. Churchill, and Joel W. Eastman, eds. *Maine: The Pine Tree State from Pre-history to the Present.* Orono: University of Maine Press, 1995.

Kemble, John Haskell. *San Francisco Bay: A Pictorial Maritime History.* Ithaca, NY: Cornell Maritime Press, 1957.

Lloyd, B.E. *Lights and Shades in San Francisco.* San Francisco: A.L. Bancroft and Company, 1876. (Republished in 1999 by Berkeley Hills Books, Berkeley, CA.)

Locke, M. Louisa. *Maids of Misfortune: A Victorian San Francisco Mystery.* M. Louisa Locke, 2009.

Lubbock, Basil. *The Downeasters: American Deep-water Sailing Ships (1869–1929).* Glasgow: Brown, Son and Ferguson. 1929.

Lynch, Timothy G. *Beyond the Golden Gate: A Maritime History of California.* New York: The Fort Schuyler Press, 2015.

Matthews, Frederick C. *American Merchant Ships (1850–1900).* New York: Dover Publications, 1987.

McKinlay, William Laird. *The Last Voyage of the Karluk.* London: Weidenfeld and Nicolson, 1976.

Millard, Candice. *Destiny of the Republic: A Tale of Madness, Medicine and the Murder of a President.* New York: Doubleday, 2011.

Mitchell, Sir William (Ed.). *Maritime Notes and Queries: From a Record of Shipping Law and Usage,* Vol. 3, 1875. London: Spottiswoode and Co., 1898.

Owen, Henry Wilson. *History of Bath.* Bath, ME: The Times Company, 1936.

Rudiak-Gould, Peter. *Surviving Paradise.* New York: Union Square Press, 2009.

Sims, Michael. *Arthur and Sherlock: Conan Doyle and the Creation of Holmes.* New York: Bloomsbury, 2017.

Smith, Marion Jacques. *A Brief History of Education in Bath, Maine.* Bath, ME: Undated study.

———. *A History of Maine, from Wilderness to Statehood.* Freeport, ME: The Bond Wheelwright Company, 1949.

Tobin, Jack A. *Stories from the Marshall Islands*. Honolulu: University of Hawaii Press, 2002.

White, Richard. *The Republic for Which It Stands: The United States during Reconstruction and the Gilded Age (1865–1896)*. Oxford: Oxford University Press, 2017.

Winchester, Simon. *Krakatoa: The Day the World Exploded, August 27, 1883*. London: Viking, 2003.

———. *Pacific*. New York: HarperCollins, 2015.